Meditation for Modern Life

Meditation for Modern Life

Overcoming Stress, Anxiety, and Burnout
in the Digital Age

Aria Blake

MINDFUL PAGES

Published in 2023

ISBN: 9789358814101 (PB)
ISBN: 9789358813968 (eBook)

Published by

Mindful Pages
Imprint of Alpha Editions LLC
312 W. 2nd St #1834
Casper, WY 82601, USA

Contents

Introduction

In an era defined by the ceaseless hum of notifications, the relentless glow of screens, and the unending rush of modern life, it's easy to feel overwhelmed. Our digital age has brought us tremendous convenience, connectivity, and opportunities. Still, it has also ushered in a new set of challenges—stress, anxiety, and burnout have become unwelcome companions in the fast-paced world we navigate daily. It's a paradox: while technology has promised us more leisure time, it often feels as if we have less. The very tools designed to simplify our lives can, at times, make them more complex.

This book, "Meditation for Modern Life: Overcoming Stress, Anxiety, and Burnout in the Digital Age," invites you to explore a path to tranquillity and resilience amid the chaos. It's a journey through the ancient wisdom of meditation, reimagined and tailored to meet the unique demands of our time. With the rise of smartphones and the constant connectivity of the internet, it's vital that we adapt our approach to managing stress and preserving our mental and emotional well-being.

We'll delve into the science behind meditation, understanding how this practice can transform your brain and body. But this book goes beyond the theoretical—our primary goal is to equip you with a toolkit of practical meditation techniques designed specifically for the challenges of modern life.

We'll explore mindfulness, breathing exercises, and digital detox practices that will help you regain control over your thoughts and emotions. You'll learn how to use these techniques to find calm amid the chaos, no matter where you are or what's happening in your life.

But meditation isn't just about relaxation; it's a gateway to holistic wellness. In these pages, you'll discover the interconnectedness of stress, nutrition, exercise, and sleep. You'll also learn how to communicate mindfully, balance your professional and personal life, and find purpose and meaning in a world that often seems relentless.

As we embark on this journey together, remember that you're not alone. The digital age affects us all, and each of us can benefit from the timeless wisdom of meditation in a modern context. Whether you're a seasoned meditator or a complete novice, this book offers a path to better understanding yourself, your environment, and the world you navigate.

So, let's take a deep breath, and begin. Your adventure into meditation for modern life starts now. Together, we'll uncover the tools and insights needed to conquer stress, anxiety, and burnout and to embrace a more balanced, mindful, and purposeful existence in the digital age.

Are you ready to reclaim your peace and find serenity amidst the modern chaos? Let's begin.

Understanding Stress, Anxiety, and Burnout

The modern age, often lauded for its advancements and conveniences, has also ushered in a new era of stress, anxiety, and burnout. These afflictions, now seemingly pervasive in our daily lives, can be likened to shadowy companions that, despite their unwelcome presence, have become deeply ingrained in the human experience. Understanding the origins, manifestations, and consequences of stress, anxiety, and burnout in the modern world is essential if we are to combat them effectively.

The Digital Dilemma

In the not-so-distant past, our forebears could enjoy moments of solitude, leisurely reading a book, or strolling through the park without the persistent hum of notifications and the weight of an ever-connected world bearing down upon them. Today, the digital age, characterized by the omnipresence of smartphones, constant email alerts, and the insatiable appetite for social media, has brought about a paradigm shift in the way we live and communicate. While it has its undeniable merits, this new age has also introduced an array of stressors that were once foreign to the human psyche.

In this modern world, we are expected to be not only productive at work but also continuously responsive to the demands of our online lives. The boundary between work and personal time blurs as our smartphones beckon us to respond to emails, messages, and work-related issues at all hours. This relentless connectivity and pressure to be available 24/7 contribute to a sense of chronic stress. It's as if we are all sprinting in a never-ending race, without the luxury of a finish line.

The Stress Paradox

Stress, in its essence, is not inherently harmful. In fact, it is a natural, evolutionary response that enabled our ancestors to survive and thrive in a world fraught with dangers. The "fight or flight" response, initiated by the release of stress hormones like cortisol and adrenaline, helped early humans react quickly to life-threatening situations.

However, the stressors our ancestors faced were primarily physical threats, such as predators or environmental dangers. In contrast, our modern world is inundated with psychological stressors, many of which are chronic and intangible. This disconnect between the body's innate stress response and the abstract, ongoing stressors of the digital age leads to a paradox: stress, which was once a life-saving mechanism, is now one of the leading causes of health problems and mental distress.

The Anxiety Epidemic

Anxiety, like stress, is a normal emotional response to certain situations. It's the apprehension and unease one feels when facing a challenging task, making a decision, or confronting the unknown. In moderation, anxiety can be motivating and even protective. However, in the modern age, anxiety often transcends healthy bounds and transforms into an insidious force that seeps into everyday life.

The digital age, with its endless stream of news and social media updates, contributes to the chronic anxiety that many individuals experience. The constant barrage of information and the fear of missing out (FOMO) can trigger feelings of inadequacy, inadequacy, and an insatiable need to be connected. The world becomes an overwhelming place, and restlessness and worry become constant companions.

Burnout: The Silent Culprit

Burnout, the most sinister of this unholy trio, is often overlooked. While stress and anxiety manifest visibly, burnout creeps in silently, like a thief in the night. It is a state of emotional, physical, and mental exhaustion brought on by prolonged, unrelenting stress. Burnout leads to a sense of hopelessness, detachment, and a decrease in one's sense of accomplishment. The once-passionate individual becomes disillusioned and disengaged.

The digital age, with its unyielding work demands, increased screen time, and blurred boundaries between personal and professional life, has created fertile ground for burnout to flourish. Many individuals are unknowingly spiralling into this abyss, numbing themselves to the overwhelming weight of their responsibilities.

The Consequences of Modern Stress

The consequences of the modern stress, anxiety, and burnout are far-reaching and, often, insidious. Physically, stress can manifest in various ways, from headaches and digestive issues to more severe conditions such as cardiovascular disease, weakened immune systems, and chronic pain. On the mental and emotional fronts, stress and anxiety can lead to symptoms of depression, panic disorders, and feelings of helplessness.

Burnout, in particular, can have a profound impact on one's life. It not only affects an individual's overall well-being but also seeps into their relationships and work performance. Personal relationships can suffer as burnout makes individuals less emotionally available, while work performance may deteriorate due to reduced motivation and engagement.

In the broader societal context, the prevalence of stress, anxiety, and burnout leads to increased healthcare costs, decreased work productivity, and a general erosion of well-being. It's a silent epidemic that affects individuals, families, and entire communities.

The Need for a Paradigm Shift

The realization that stress, anxiety, and burnout are widespread and often accepted as the norm in the modern age necessitates a paradigm shift. It's time to recognize that our digital advancements, while groundbreaking in many ways, have also challenged our capacity to lead balanced, fulfilling lives. The constant connectivity and pressure to perform at an unsustainable pace are not the way forward.

It's imperative that we develop a new understanding of stress, anxiety, and burnout—one that acknowledges the unique challenges of our time. This understanding is the first step toward overcoming these modern afflictions and finding a more harmonious way to live in the digital age.

In the chapters that follow, we will delve deeper into the science of meditation and mindfulness as tools to confront and conquer stress, anxiety, and burnout in the modern world. By understanding the roots of these issues and exploring practical techniques, we can reclaim our well-being and peace of mind in a fast-paced, interconnected, and ever-evolving society.

The journey begins with the realization that we are not alone in our struggles. Stress, anxiety, and burnout are shared experiences, and through a combination of insight, self-care, and mindfulness, we can address these challenges head-on. The digital age may have introduced us to new stressors, but it also provides us with the tools to combat them effectively.

As we move forward, let's remember that understanding is the first step to change. The digital age need not be defined solely by stress, anxiety, and burnout. It can also be an era of profound personal growth, fulfilment, and well-being. By exploring the strategies and insights offered in this book, we set out on a path toward a more balanced, mindful, and peaceful existence in our modern world.

The Power of Meditation: A Tool for Modern Living

In a world characterized by perpetual motion and relentless stimuli, the power of meditation emerges as a potent tool for modern living. As the digital age reshapes the way we interact with the world, individuals from all walks of life are increasingly seeking refuge from the chaos and stress that accompanies this new era. Meditation, once considered a niche practice, has entered the mainstream as a transformative tool to navigate the challenges of the modern age. Its ability to promote mental and emotional well-being, enhance focus and productivity, and foster a profound sense of inner peace makes it a compelling resource for those seeking balance and tranquility amidst the chaos. This exploration delves into the power of meditation and its relevance in today's fast-paced, interconnected world.

Meditation: An Ancient Practice for Modern Times

Meditation is not a new phenomenon. It is a practice with roots that extend thousands of years into human history, spanning cultures and traditions worldwide. From the Vipassana meditation of Buddhism to the transcendental meditation techniques of Hinduism and the mindfulness practices of the Zen tradition, meditation has a rich and diverse history. It has been used for centuries as a means of gaining insight, deepening one's spiritual connection, and achieving a state of inner peace.

Despite its ancient origins, meditation's popularity has surged in recent years, with people from various backgrounds embracing it as a way to navigate the demands and complexities of modern living. This renaissance is driven, in part, by the recognition that our fast-paced, technology-driven world has brought with it an array of unique challenges, including heightened stress, anxiety, and a constant influx of information.

The Science Behind Meditation

Meditation is often perceived as a mystical or esoteric practice. However, the power of meditation is firmly grounded in scientific principles. Numerous studies have explored the effects of meditation on the human brain and body, revealing a profound and positive impact on physical and mental health.

One of the key physiological changes that occur during meditation is the activation of the parasympathetic nervous system, which is responsible for the "rest and digest" response. This activation leads to a reduction in the release of stress hormones, such as cortisol, and a decrease in heart rate and blood pressure. As a result, meditation can effectively counteract the physiological effects of stress, promoting relaxation and a sense of calm.

Meditation also has a remarkable impact on the brain. Through techniques like functional magnetic resonance imaging (fMRI) and electroencephalography (EEG), researchers have observed changes in brain structure and function in individuals who meditate regularly. One of the most studied areas of the brain is the prefrontal cortex, which is associated with attention, self-awareness, and emotional regulation. Meditation has been shown to increase the activity and connectivity of this region, leading to improved focus, emotional balance, and overall well-being.

Furthermore, meditation is known to promote neuroplasticity, the brain's ability to reorganize and adapt to new experiences. This means that, even in the digital age, when our brains are bombarded with information and stimuli, meditation can help us train our minds to become more resilient, adaptable, and focused.

Mindfulness Meditation: Staying Present in a Fast-Paced World

One of the most popular and accessible forms of meditation in the modern age is mindfulness meditation. Mindfulness, rooted in Buddhist tradition, revolves around the practice of paying deliberate, non-judgmental attention to the present moment. It encourages individuals to observe their thoughts, emotions, and sensations without attachment or judgment.

In a world that constantly demands our attention and encourages multitasking, mindfulness meditation offers a powerful counterbalance. By learning to stay present in each moment, we can reduce the impact of stress and anxiety. Rather than ruminating on past events or worrying about the future, mindfulness helps us appreciate the beauty and significance of each instant.

As we engage in mindfulness meditation, we gradually learn to detach from our racing thoughts and emotions. This detachment allows us to respond to life's challenges with greater composure and clarity. We become less reactive and more in control of our responses, leading to improved emotional regulation and decision-making.

Breathing Techniques: Calming the Anxious Mind

Breathing is a fundamental aspect of life, but it often goes unnoticed. We breathe thousands of times each day without consciously considering the act. However, the power of meditation lies in its ability to transform something as ordinary as breathing into a source of inner calm and clarity.

Breathing techniques, such as diaphragmatic breathing and the 4-7-8 technique, are simple yet powerful tools for managing stress and anxiety. These techniques emphasize conscious control of the breath, encouraging deep, slow, and deliberate inhalations and exhalations.

By focusing on the breath, individuals can activate the parasympathetic nervous system, initiating the relaxation response. This shift from the "fight or flight" mode to the "rest and digest" mode can quickly alleviate feelings of anxiety and stress. It's a technique that can be practiced anytime and anywhere, making it particularly valuable in the modern age when moments of respite can be scarce.

Body Scan Meditation: Releasing Tension and Stress

The physical toll of stress and anxiety is often underestimated. Chronic stress can manifest as muscle tension, headaches, and even chronic pain conditions. Body scan meditation is a powerful technique that allows individuals to tune into their bodies and identify areas of tension or discomfort.

In a body scan meditation, practitioners mentally scan their bodies from head to toe, paying close attention to any sensations they encounter. This process of introspection can reveal areas of tension and stress that often go unnoticed in the hustle and bustle of daily life.

Once these areas are identified, individuals can use mindfulness and relaxation techniques to release tension and reduce physical discomfort. The power of body scan meditation lies in its ability to unite the mind and body, providing a holistic approach to stress management.

Walking Meditation: Finding Peace in Motion

In a world that values constant motion and productivity, finding moments of stillness can be challenging. Traditional seated meditation practices might not align with the preferences or schedules of many individuals. This is where walking meditation, or "kinhin" in the Zen tradition, comes into play.

Walking meditation transforms a simple act into a mindful practice. It involves walking slowly and deliberately, paying close attention to each step and the sensations associated with it. This form of meditation can be particularly beneficial for those who find it difficult to sit still for extended periods or who simply enjoy the act of walking.

The power of walking meditation lies in its ability to bridge the gap between the fast-paced world we live in and the inner peace we seek. It encourages a state of mindfulness while on the move, allowing individuals to experience tranquillity even in the midst of physical activity.

Digital Detox Meditation: Reclaiming Your Time and Attention

In a world dominated by screens and devices, digital detox meditation offers a means of regaining control over our relationship with technology. The power of this form of meditation is twofold: it helps individuals recognize and address the addictive nature of digital devices, and it offers techniques for reducing screen time and refocusing attention on the present moment.

Digital detox meditation often begins with self-reflection. Individuals assess the amount of time they spend on screens and consider the impact of this behaviour on their mental and emotional well-being. This awareness can serve as a powerful motivator for change.

Meditation techniques can then be used to gradually reduce screen time and foster mindfulness. Simple practices, such as setting specific periods for screen use, practicing mindful phone checks, and engaging in tech-free activities, allow individuals to reclaim their time and attention. Digital detox meditation empowers individuals to be the masters of their devices rather than the other way around.

Meditation for Modern Life: Embracing Balance and Tranquillity

Meditation is more than a passive escape from the stresses of modern life; it is an active tool that equips individuals to navigate this digital age with resilience and composure. In today's fast-paced world, meditation stands as a pillar of strength and self-awareness, offering an antidote to the ceaseless stimuli and pressures of the digital age.

As scientific research continues to illuminate the profound effects of meditation on the brain and body, its potential as a tool for modern living becomes increasingly apparent. It is not a mystical or esoteric practice; it is a practical and accessible means of promoting mental and emotional well-being, enhancing focus and productivity, and fostering a profound sense of inner peace.

While the challenges of the digital age are real and pervasive, so too is the power of meditation to transform lives. By embracing meditation as a daily practice, individuals can find the balance and tranquillity they seek in a world that often seems overwhelming. It is a tool that empowers individuals to take control of their well-being, reducing stress and anxiety while promoting a sense of inner peace and clarity.

In the chapters that follow, we will explore the practical aspects of incorporating meditation into modern life. We will delve into the art of creating a consistent meditation practice, as well as how to overcome common challenges and resistance. We will also explore the relationship between meditation and other facets of holistic wellness, such as nutrition, exercise, and sleep.

Meditation for modern living is not a solitary endeavour; it is a journey that individuals embark upon with the support and camaraderie of countless others who also seek balance and tranquillity. It is a journey filled with insights, revelations, and a profound sense of connection with the world and oneself.

As we continue to navigate the digital age, let us remember the enduring power of meditation to promote well-being, reduce stress, and offer a path to profound inner peace. The challenges of modern living may be significant, but so too is the power of meditation to help us thrive in this fast-paced, interconnected world.

Stress, anxiety, and burnout have become ubiquitous terms in our modern lexicon. In the fast-paced, interconnected world we navigate daily, these experiences have woven themselves into the fabric of our lives, shaping our well-being and relationships. While we may use these terms frequently, truly comprehending their origins, manifestations, and consequences is essential for effectively addressing and mitigating their impact.

This in-depth exploration takes us beyond the surface of stress, anxiety, and burnout, diving deep into their underlying dynamics, intricacies, and the profound influence they exert on our physical and mental health.

The Complex Tapestry of Stress

Stress, in its purest form, is a physiological and psychological response that has been hardwired into our biology for millennia. It's the reaction that mobilizes our bodies to deal with perceived threats or challenges. In simpler times, our ancestors encountered physical dangers like predators or scarcity of resources, and the "fight or flight" response, triggered by stress, helped them survive.

However, the modern age has reshaped the nature of stressors. No longer are our threats primarily physical; they've evolved into complex, chronic, and often psychological stressors. In today's world, stressors can range from financial worries and work pressures to the constant stream of information and stimuli we encounter through digital devices.

This transformation creates a paradox. Stress, which was once a life-preserving mechanism, has now become a chief contributor to health problems and mental distress. The body's natural response designed to protect us from immediate physical danger has become a constant presence in our lives.

The All-Encompassing Nature of Anxiety

While stress is the precursor, anxiety is its close companion, accompanying individuals through the ups and downs of modern life. Anxiety is the anticipatory worry, the feeling of unease or apprehension that often precedes a stressful event or even occurs in the absence of an immediate stressor.

The digital age has ushered in a tidal wave of anxiety, primarily due to the incessant flow of information and the interconnectedness of our lives. The constant notifications, news alerts, and the pressure to stay informed can be overwhelming, leaving us in a state of perpetual vigilance. This anticipatory anxiety, while designed to prepare us for potential dangers, has taken root in the form of generalized anxiety and chronic worry.

Individuals may find themselves preoccupied with what-ifs and worst-case scenarios, leading to mental exhaustion and a heightened sense of vulnerability. The incessant rumination on future events, combined with the stressors of daily life, can create a perfect storm of anxiety.

Burnout: The Silent Intruder

If stress is the precursor and anxiety is the relentless companion, burnout is the silent intruder that often goes unnoticed until it has already taken a significant toll. Burnout is the state of emotional, physical, and mental exhaustion that results from prolonged, unrelenting stress. It erodes one's sense of accomplishment, enthusiasm, and connection to their work or activities.

In the modern age, burnout has become an epidemic that stealthily infiltrates the lives of individuals, particularly in high-demand professions. The digital age, with its perpetually connected nature, blurs the lines between personal and professional life. This constant accessibility has allowed stress to seep into every corner of our lives, giving burnout ample room to thrive.

Those affected by burnout often experience a pervasive sense of disillusionment, detachment, and a marked decrease in their effectiveness and motivation. It's a phenomenon that affects not only the individual but also their work, relationships, and overall well-being.

The Consequences of Modern Stress

The consequences of modern stress are far-reaching and often insidious. Physically, stress can manifest in various ways, from common complaints like headaches, digestive issues, and muscle tension to more serious health conditions such as cardiovascular disease, weakened immune systems, and chronic pain. The physical impact of stress on the body should not be underestimated, as it can lead to a cascade of health issues.

Mentally and emotionally, the weight of modern stress can be even more profound. Stress and anxiety are well-known precursors to mental health conditions like depression, panic disorders, and even post-traumatic stress disorder. The constant state of vigilance and anticipation that anxiety induces can lead to a constant state of alertness that taxes the mind and the emotions.

Burnout, in particular, affects not just the individual but also the broader societal context. The prevalence of burnout in the workplace leads to decreased productivity, absenteeism, and increased healthcare costs. It can have a ripple effect on the workforce and the economy, with burnout costing billions of dollars annually in lost productivity.

The Interconnectedness of Stress, Anxiety, and Burnout

While stress, anxiety, and burnout are distinct concepts, they are intricately interconnected and often feed into one another. Stress, as the primary instigator, creates a fertile ground for the development of anxiety. Chronic stressors heighten anticipatory anxiety and lead to rumination on potential threats or problems.

As anxiety deepens and becomes chronic, it, in turn, contributes to the development of burnout. The constant sense of vigilance and worry takes a toll on one's emotional and physical resources, ultimately leading to exhaustion and a sense of detachment from work and life in general.

Furthermore, the constant state of alertness and overstimulation brought on by the digital age exacerbates this cycle. The 24/7 access to work-related matters, combined with the constant influx of information through digital devices, creates a relentless and overwhelming environment that keeps the cycle of stress, anxiety, and burnout in motion.

The Digital Age: A Double-Edged Sword

The digital age, with its technological marvels and promises of convenience and connectivity, is both a boon and a bane. On one hand, it has revolutionized the way we communicate, access information, and conduct our daily lives. On the other hand, it has ushered in an era where stressors are increasingly abstract, digital, and chronic.

The constant connectivity brought on by the digital age poses a unique challenge to our stress response. The inability to disconnect from work, the barrage of notifications, and the pervasive pressure to respond instantly to messages create a state of perpetual vigilance and reactivity. This constant state of alertness taxes our stress response systems and can lead to a chronic state of stress.

Moreover, the digital age has transformed our understanding of leisure time. What was once a respite from work has become an extension of it, as individuals often find themselves tethered to their devices and email inboxes, even during moments of relaxation. This inability to truly unwind perpetuates stress and contributes to the burnout that plagues many in the modern world.

Recognizing the Signs

In order to address and mitigate the effects of stress, anxiety, and burnout in the digital age, it is crucial to recognize the signs and symptoms of these conditions. Awareness is the first step towards intervention and prevention.

For stress, signs may include an increased heart rate, muscle tension, irritability, and difficulty sleeping. It's important to note that not all stress is harmful; some stress is normal and even beneficial. The key is recognizing when stress crosses the threshold into chronic or overwhelming territory.

Anxiety often manifests as excessive worry, restlessness, an inability to concentrate, and physical symptoms such as trembling or shortness of breath. It is essential to acknowledge when anxiety begins to affect daily life and well-being significantly

The Digital Age Dilemma: Causes and Impact on Modern Society

The digital age, marked by the rapid advancement of technology and the pervasive integration of digital devices into every aspect of our lives, has ushered in an era of unprecedented convenience and connectivity. From the convenience of smartphones to the power of the internet, the digital age has transformed the way we communicate, work, and access information. Yet, this digital revolution has also introduced myriad challenges and dilemmas that impact individuals, society, and culture. This exploration delves into the causes of the digital age dilemma and examines its profound impact on our modern world.

The Digital Revolution: A Brief Overview

Before delving into the dilemmas the digital age poses, it's essential to provide context by understanding the revolutionary changes it has brought to our lives. The digital revolution, also known as the Information Age, began in the latter half of the 20th century with the development of digital technology and the widespread use of computers. Over the years, it has evolved into an era characterized by the following key developments:

The Internet: The development of the World Wide Web in the 1990s marked a pivotal moment in human history. It allowed information to be shared globally, rapidly altering the way we access knowledge, communicate, and conduct business.

Personal Computing: The advent of personal computers brought digital capabilities to individuals' homes. This not only transformed the way we work but also laid the foundation for the development of countless digital devices.

Smartphones: The introduction of smartphones, led by Apple's iPhone in 2007, ushered in a new era of mobile computing. These devices became essential tools for communication, entertainment, and productivity.

Social Media: The rise of social media platforms, like Facebook, Twitter, and Instagram, revolutionized how we connect with others and share our lives online. These platforms have become integral to modern social interactions.

Big Data and Analytics: The ability to collect, store, and analyze massive amounts of data has transformed industries and the way we make decisions. It has implications in business, healthcare, and government, among others.

Artificial Intelligence: AI and machine learning have rapidly evolved, impacting areas like autonomous vehicles, healthcare, and personal digital assistants, such as Siri and Alexa.

Internet of Things (IoT): Everyday objects are now connected to the internet, enabling smart homes, wearable devices, and enhanced industrial processes.

The digital revolution has undeniably brought numerous benefits, including increased efficiency, access to information, and enhanced communication. However, with these advancements come a range of challenges and dilemmas that deserve careful consideration.

The Digital Age Dilemma: Causes and Complexities

The digital age dilemma encompasses a multitude of challenges that span from personal well-being to societal impact. Several key causes and complexities contribute to this dilemma:

Information Overload:

> **The Infinite Stream of Data:** The internet has democratized information, enabling anyone with an internet connection to access vast amounts of data. While this is a boon for knowledge, it has also led to information overload. The relentless flow of news, emails, notifications, and social media updates can be overwhelming and mentally exhausting.

> **Filter Bubbles:** Algorithms used by search engines and social media platforms personalize the content users see, often reinforcing pre-existing beliefs and limiting exposure to diverse perspectives. This phenomenon is referred to as a "filter bubble" and can contribute to echo chambers and the spread of misinformation.

Constant Connectivity:

The Always-On Culture: The digital age has led to a culture of constant connectivity. The ubiquity of smartphones means that individuals are accessible around the clock, often blurring the boundaries between work and personal life. This 24/7 availability can lead to stress, exhaustion, and burnout.

FOMO (Fear of Missing Out): The fear of missing out on social events, news, or opportunities, often exacerbated by social media, can lead to anxiety and the compulsion to constantly check devices. This compulsion can interfere with genuine experiences and hinder the ability to be fully present in the moment.

Privacy Concerns:

Data Collection: Companies and organizations collect extensive data on individuals without their explicit consent or knowledge. This has raised significant concerns about personal privacy and the potential misuse of data.

Surveillance: The digital age has seen a rise in surveillance by governments and private entities. The extensive monitoring of individuals' online activities has implications for civil liberties and personal freedom.

Digital Addiction:

Tech Dependence: The allure of digital devices and the constant stimulation they offer can lead to addiction-like behaviors. Individuals may find it difficult to detach from screens and experience withdrawal symptoms when attempting to do so.

Internet Gaming Disorder: Some individuals develop problematic patterns of gaming behavior, leading to the recognition of conditions like internet gaming disorder as a mental health concern.

Mental Health Impact:

Digital Stress: The digital age has introduced new stressors, such as the pressure to be constantly available, cyberbullying, and the emotional toll of social media. These stressors can have a detrimental impact on mental health.

Isolation and Loneliness: Paradoxically, the digital age, despite its connectivity, has been associated with increased feelings of isolation and loneliness. Social media interactions, while providing a sense of connection, can be shallow and lack the depth of face-to-face relationships.

Disruption of Traditional Industries:

Economic Shifts: The digital age has disrupted traditional industries, causing job displacement in some sectors while creating new opportunities in others. This shift raises questions about workforce adaptability and economic inequality.

Copyright and Intellectual Property: The ease of digital reproduction and distribution has raised copyright and intellectual property issues. Protecting the rights of creators in a digital world is a complex and ongoing challenge.

Cybersecurity Concerns:

Cyberattacks: The digital age has witnessed a surge, with hackers targeting individuals, businesses, and governments. These attacks can result in data breaches, financial losses, and even threats to national security.

Data Vulnerability: With the increasing amount of personal data stored online, individuals are more susceptible to identity theft and other cybercrimes. Protecting personal information is a critical concern.

Impact on Social Interactions:

Shifting Social Norms: The digital age has changed the way we interact with others, from the rise of online dating to the prevalence of virtual gatherings. These changes impact traditional social norms and etiquette.

Digital Disconnection: While digital technology connects us to a global audience, it can also lead to disconnection from our immediate surroundings. The overuse of digital devices in social settings can hinder genuine interpersonal connections.

Environmental Consequences:

E-Waste: The proliferation of digital devices contributes to electronic waste (e-waste), which poses environmental challenges in terms of disposal and recycling.

Energy Consumption: The data centers and infrastructure required to support the digital age have substantial energy demands, leading to concerns about sustainability and environmental impact.

Digital Divide:

Access Disparities: While digital technology has transformed many aspects of life, it has also revealed disparities in access. Not everyone has equal access to the internet, leaving marginalized communities at a disadvantage in education, employment, and social participation.

Impact on Modern Society: A Deeper Dive

The digital age's impact on modern society is profound, touching nearly every facet of our lives. It's essential to delve deeper into the effects, both positive and negative, that this revolution has wrought.

Communication and Connectivity:

Positive Impact: The digital age has facilitated global communication, enabling individuals to connect with loved ones, collaborate across borders, and access information from around the world. Social media platforms, in particular, have connected people and provided a voice to those who previously may not have had one.

Negative Impact: While connectivity has its advantages, it has also led to a decline in face-to-face interactions and, in some cases, shallow online relationships. The ease of communication can also lead to cyberbullying, harassment, and the spread of hate speech.

Work and Productivity:

Positive Impact: The digital age has transformed the workplace, enabling remote work, flexible hours, and enhanced productivity through digital tools and collaboration platforms. It has also created new job opportunities in the tech and digital sectors.

Negative Impact: The constant connectivity of the digital age has blurred the lines between work and personal life, contributing to burnout and stress. The expectation of being available at all hours can lead to a diminished work-life balance.

Education and Learning:

Positive Impact: Digital technology has revolutionized education, providing online courses, resources, and interactive learning experiences. It has democratized access to knowledge and enabled lifelong learning.

Negative Impact: The reliance on digital devices for education can exacerbate inequalities, as not all students have access to the necessary technology. It has also raised concerns about the quality of online education and the potential for cheating and plagiarism.

Entertainment and Media:

Positive Impact: The digital age has made entertainment and media more accessible, allowing individuals to stream movies, music, and television shows on-demand. It has also empowered independent creators to share their work with a global audience.

Negative Impact: The availability of endless digital entertainment can lead to issues of addiction, excessive screen time, and a decline in physical activity. The digital age has disrupted traditional media industries, leading to concerns about the future of journalism and content creation.

Healthcare and Medicine:

Positive Impact: Digital technology has advanced healthcare through telemedicine, electronic health records, and wearable devices that monitor health metrics. It has improved patient care, research, and diagnosis.

Negative Impact: The collection and storage of personal health data raise privacy concerns, as well as the potential for data breaches. There are also disparities in access to digital healthcare resources, impacting underserved communities.

Politics and Activism:

Positive Impact: The digital age has empowered individuals to engage in political discourse, activism, and social change. Social media platforms have played a pivotal role in organizing movements and raising awareness.

Negative Impact: The spread of misinformation and the echo chamber effect on social media can polarize political discourse and hinder productive dialogue. There are also concerns about the influence of digital platforms on elections and political manipulation.

Shopping and Commerce:

Positive Impact: Online shopping and e-commerce have revolutionized the retail industry, offering convenience and a vast array of products. It has also created opportunities for small businesses to reach a global market.

Negative Impact: The dominance of e-commerce giants can stifle competition and traditional brick-and-mortar businesses. It has also led to concerns about data privacy and security in online transactions.

Transportation and Mobility:

Positive Impact: Ride-sharing services and innovations in transportation have provided convenient and flexible mobility options. Electric vehicles and advancements in autonomous driving promise a more sustainable and efficient future.

Negative Impact: The proliferation of ride-sharing has raised concerns about congestion and its environmental impact. Autonomous vehicles also raise questions about job displacement and the ethical challenges of self-driving technology.

Environment and Sustainability:

Positive Impact: Digital technology has the potential to address environmental challenges, with innovations in renewable energy, smart cities, and sustainable agriculture. The digital age can enhance environmental monitoring and conservation efforts.

Negative Impact: The energy consumption of data centers and electronic devices contributes to carbon emissions. The production and disposal of e-waste pose environmental challenges. The digital age has also increased energy demands and resource use.

Privacy and Security: -

Positive Impact: Digital encryption and cybersecurity measures are crucial for protecting personal information and ensuring online security. The advancement of technology has led to greater awareness of the need for data privacy.

Negative Impact: The digital age has raised significant concerns about data breaches, identity theft, and the vulnerability of personal information. Surveillance by both governmental and corporate entities has led to debates over civil liberties and the erosion of privacy.

The Future of the Digital Age: Navigating the Dilemma

As we navigate the digital age and grapple with its dilemmas, it's essential to consider how society and individuals can adapt to the challenges while harnessing the benefits. The future of the digital age will likely involve addressing these dilemmas through various means:

Education and Digital Literacy:

Promoting Critical Thinking: Teaching critical thinking skills and media literacy is crucial in helping individuals navigate the vast sea of information and discern credible sources from misinformation.

Cybersecurity Awareness: Education about online safety and privacy is vital, empowering individuals to protect themselves and their data.

Regulation and Policy:

Data Privacy Laws: Governments and regulatory bodies must establish and enforce data privacy laws, giving individuals greater control over their personal information.

Anti-Monopoly Measures: Regulatory action may be necessary to address the dominance of tech giants and ensure fair competition.

Ethical Technology Design:

Responsible Tech Development: Technology companies should prioritize the ethical development of their products, considering the impact on individuals' mental health and well-being.

User-Centered Design: Prioritizing user experience and well-being over screen time and engagement metrics can lead to more thoughtful and responsible design.

Digital Detox and Balance:

Mindful Technology Use: Encouraging individuals to be mindful of their digital consumption and periodically disconnect from screens is essential for mental health.

Digital Sabbaticals: Extended breaks from digital devices and social media can help individuals reset and regain perspective.

Access and Inclusivity:

Digital Inclusion: Efforts must be made to bridge the digital divide, ensuring that underserved communities have access to the internet and digital resources.

Accessibility: The design of digital technology should prioritize accessibility for individuals with disabilities to ensure inclusivity.

Environmental Responsibility:

> **Sustainable Practices:** Companies and individuals can adopt sustainable practices in the production, use, and disposal of digital devices to reduce e-waste and energy consumption.

> **Renewable Energy:** Transitioning data centers to renewable energy sources can help reduce the environmental impact of digital technology.

Mental Health and Well-Being:

> **Digital Mindfulness:** Practices like digital detox, screen time management, and meditation can promote mental health and well-being in the digital age.

> **Mental Health Support:** Access to mental health resources and services should be readily available to address the stressors of the digital age.

Responsible Consumption and Activism:

> **Conscious Consumerism:** Individuals can make informed choices about the digital products and services they use, considering their ethical and environmental impact.

> **Digital Activism:** Social media and online platforms can be harnessed for social and environmental activism, raising awareness and advocating for positive change.

The digital age dilemma is complex and multifaceted, reflecting both the remarkable opportunities and pressing challenges of the digital era. Navigating this dilemma requires a collective effort that encompasses individuals, technology companies, policymakers, and society at large. It is through careful consideration, ethical decision-making, and responsible use of technology that we can harness the benefits of the digital age while addressing its dilemmas and ensuring a brighter future for all.

The Mind-Body Connection: How Stress Affects Your Health

In the intricate and harmonious symphony that is the human body, the connection between the mind and the body plays a pivotal role. It's a connection that influences not only our mental and emotional well-being but also our physical health. At the heart of this intricate relationship is the phenomenon of stress and its profound impact on our bodies. Stress, while often seen as a mental or emotional state, has the power to infiltrate our physiology, influencing everything from our immune system to our cardiovascular health. It's a remarkable and often sobering reminder that the mind and body are not separate entities but rather two intimately intertwined facets of our existence.

When we think of stress, we tend to picture a worried mind or a racing heart, but it goes much deeper than that. Stress triggers a physiological response, known as the "fight or flight" response, which readies the body to face a perceived threat. In our evolutionary history, this response served us well when confronted with predators or other immediate dangers. However, in the modern world, our stressors have evolved. We're no longer outrunning predators but juggling deadlines, bills, and a constant barrage of digital notifications. The "fight or flight" response, designed for acute, life-threatening situations, is now engaged chronically.

One of the most immediate ways stress affects our health is through the release of stress hormones, particularly cortisol. This hormone serves as the body's alarm system, alerting it to danger and preparing it for action. However, when stress becomes a constant companion, so does cortisol, leading to a cascade of physical consequences. Elevated cortisol levels have been linked to a range of health issues, including increased blood pressure, impaired cognitive function, and a weakened immune system. It's as if the body is in a constant state of readiness, which can be taxing on its resources.

The impact of chronic stress isn't limited to cortisol alone. Our immune system, which typically protects us from illnesses and infections, can become compromised under prolonged stress. This means that individuals under persistent stress are more susceptible to infections and may take longer to recover from illnesses. Moreover, stress can exacerbate inflammatory responses, contributing to conditions like chronic inflammation, which has been associated with a range of diseases, including heart disease, diabetes, and even cancer.

One area where the mind-body connection is particularly apparent is in the realm of mental health. Stress is a well-known contributor to anxiety and depression. The constant activation of the "fight or flight" response can lead to imbalances in neurotransmitters like serotonin and dopamine, which are essential for regulating mood. Additionally, the emotional toll of chronic stress can lead to a cycle of negative thinking and self-doubt, deepening the experience of anxiety and depression.

Perhaps one of the most tangible ways stress affects the body is through the cardiovascular system. Chronic stress can lead to the constriction of blood vessels and an increase in heart rate and blood pressure. This places additional strain on the heart and arteries, increasing the risk of heart disease. Stress has been linked to conditions like hypertension, atherosclerosis, and even heart attacks. The connection between chronic stress and cardiovascular health is a stark reminder that our mental and emotional well-being can have life-or-death implications.

Digestion, too, is intricately connected to stress. The body's response to stress includes the redirection of blood flow away from non-essential functions like digestion. This can lead to gastrointestinal issues, including indigestion, irritable bowel syndrome (IBS), and even ulcers. Chronic stress can also impact dietary choices, with individuals often turning to comfort foods high in sugar, salt, and unhealthy fats. These dietary habits can further exacerbate health problems, contributing to obesity and other metabolic issues.

The mind-body connection also becomes apparent in the realm of chronic pain. Stress and pain share a complex relationship, where one can exacerbate the other. Chronic stress leads to the release of stress hormones, which can increase the perception of pain. In turn, chronic pain can be a significant source of stress, creating a cycle that can be challenging to break. This interplay between stress and pain highlights how our mental state can influence our physical well-being, and vice versa.

Understanding the mind-body connection and the profound influence of stress on our health underscores the importance of stress management and holistic well-being. It's a reminder that self-care isn't just about relaxation and mental health but also about preserving the health of our bodies. Mindfulness practices, meditation, physical activity, and a balanced lifestyle all play crucial roles in mitigating the effects of stress on the body. The mind and body are not separate entities; they are two facets of a whole, and acknowledging their intimate connection is a crucial step in nurturing our overall well-being

Recognizing the Signs of Stress, Anxiety, and Burnout

Imagine your body as a sophisticated alarm system, one that's evolved over millennia to protect you from harm. When you're in danger, this system kicks into action, setting off signals that can save your life. But what happens when this alarm system misfires, sounding the alert even when you're not in immediate peril? Welcome to the world of stress, anxiety, and burnout, where our intricate physiological warning system can sometimes send false alarms that we mistake for the real thing.

Stress: The Early Warning Signal

Let's begin with stress, your body's way of telling you that something's amiss. Stress is like a helpful friend who taps you on the shoulder and says, "Hey, pay attention, something's going on!" When you encounter a challenging situation—be it a looming deadline, a traffic jam, or even a thrilling rollercoaster ride—your body responds with the "fight or flight" reaction. You might notice your heart racing, your muscles tensing, and your senses sharpening. It's your body preparing to confront or flee from a perceived threat.

Stress, in moderation, can be a powerful motivator. It can help you perform at your best under pressure, keeping you alert and focused. However, when stress becomes chronic, it's like that well-intentioned friend who won't stop tapping your shoulder. Your body remains in a constant state of readiness, leading to physical symptoms such as headaches, muscle tension, sleep disturbances, and digestive issues. It's your body's way of saying, "I need a break!" Recognizing these signs can be your first step in managing stress effectively.

Anxiety: When the Alarm Won't Stop Ringing

Now, imagine that the helpful friend who taps your shoulder turns into an overzealous companion who won't let up. That's akin to what happens when stress transforms into anxiety. Anxiety is like a car alarm that keeps blaring even when there's no real threat in sight. It's the persistent worry, unease, and restlessness that can hijack your thoughts and emotions.

When anxiety takes hold, your body and mind are on high alert. You may find yourself unable to concentrate, your heart racing, and your palms sweaty. Your mind spins a never-ending reel of "what-ifs" and worst-case scenarios. It's as if your body is preparing for an imminent danger that never arrives. Recognizing anxiety involves understanding that this persistent state of alertness can disrupt your daily life, affecting everything from work and relationships to your overall well-being.

Burnout: The Silent Intruder

If stress and anxiety are like alarms you can't turn off, burnout is more like a slow and stealthy intruder. Burnout doesn't announce itself with blaring sirens; it creeps in quietly, often unnoticed, until it has already taken its toll. Burnout is the cumulative effect of chronic stress, a state of emotional, physical, and mental exhaustion that leaves you feeling disenchanted, detached, and unproductive.

Burnout is like a subtle erosion of your vitality. You might begin to lose interest in things you once loved, feel emotionally drained, and find it challenging to concentrate. The enthusiasm you once had for your work or daily activities wanes, and it's as if you're running on empty. Recognizing burnout can be particularly challenging because it can sneak up on you, disguising itself as fatigue or a lack of motivation.

The Importance of Recognition

Recognizing the signs of stress, anxiety, and burnout is the crucial first step in addressing these challenges. It's your body's way of sending an S.O.S., telling you that it's time to take action. By becoming attuned to the physical and emotional signals—ranging from muscle tension to persistent worry—you empower yourself to intervene before these issues escalate.

Understanding that stress is a natural response, anxiety can be managed, and burnout is preventable provides a foundation for reclaiming your well-being. It's a reminder that you have the power to respond to your body's signals, to take a step back, and to implement strategies for managing and reducing these responses.

In the chapters that follow, we'll delve deeper into the strategies and techniques to address stress, anxiety, and burnout in the digital age. It's a journey of self-discovery and self-care, one that allows you to regain control over your well-being. Remember, your body's alarm system is a valuable tool, but it's up to you to determine when the alarm is a false signal, and when it's time to take action for a healthier, happier you.

The Science of Meditation: Unlocking the Secrets of Mind and Body Harmony

Meditation, the ancient practice that has transcended millennia, is like a hidden treasure trove for exploring the depths of the human mind and body. At first glance, it may appear to be an activity steeped in mysticism and spirituality, but there's an ever-growing body of scientific evidence that peels away the layers of mystique to reveal the fascinating science that underpins this age-old practice. It's a journey that takes us from the realm of brain scans and biochemistry to the profound connection between the mind and the body. So, fasten your seatbelts as we embark on a journey into the science of meditation, where you'll discover the extraordinary ways this practice can transform your life.

The Brain's Dance of Neuroplasticity

Imagine the brain as a sprawling city, with intricate pathways and bustling traffic. Every thought, emotion, and sensation triggers a complex dance of neurons and synapses. This phenomenon, known as neuroplasticity, is what allows the brain to rewire and adapt, and it's at the heart of how meditation works its magic on the mind. Scientific studies using advanced imaging techniques like fMRI (functional magnetic resonance imaging) have revealed that regular meditation can actually reconfigure the brain's architecture.

One area of the brain that undergoes remarkable changes through meditation is the prefrontal cortex, often called the "CEO of the brain." It's responsible for decision-making, focus, and emotional regulation. Through meditation, this region becomes more finely tuned, leading to improved concentration and emotional stability. Researchers have also observed an increase in gray matter density in the hippocampus, associated with memory and learning, in meditation practitioners. These brain changes offer a scientific explanation for meditation's power in enhancing mental clarity and emotional well-being.

The Neurotransmitter Symphony

Within your brain, a symphony of neurotransmitters orchestrates your mood and emotions. Think of them as the conductors of your mental orchestra. Serotonin, dopamine, and endorphins, among others, influence your feelings of happiness and well-being. And here's where meditation enters the scene as the maestro. Studies have shown that meditation can boost the production of these "feel-good" neurotransmitters while reducing the levels of stress hormones like cortisol.

For instance, meditation can stimulate the release of serotonin, which plays a crucial role in regulating mood and preventing depression. It's like a natural antidepressant, minus the side effects. Dopamine, responsible for motivation and pleasure, also gets a boost during meditation, enhancing your sense of well-being. The release of endorphins during meditation, those natural painkillers and mood enhancers, creates a sense of euphoria. It's no wonder that meditators often report feeling happier and more content.

The Immune System Harmony

The connection between the mind and the body is not just about your mental state; it extends to your physical well-being as well. The immune system, your body's defense against illness and disease, is profoundly affected by your mental state. Chronic stress weakens the immune system, leaving you vulnerable to infections and diseases. Meditation acts as a soothing balm for your immune system, reducing stress and inflammation.

Research has shown that the relaxation response induced by meditation can have a profound impact on the expression of genes related to inflammation. Inflammation is at the root of numerous chronic diseases, from heart disease to cancer. By calming the body's stress response, meditation essentially helps in putting out the fires of inflammation. This is not a mystical claim; it's grounded in the scientific understanding of the intricate interplay between the mind and the immune system.

Heartfelt Harmony

The heart, often regarded as the seat of emotions, is also deeply influenced by meditation. In a world where cardiovascular diseases are a leading cause of mortality, the impact of meditation on heart health is especially significant. Meditation's ability to reduce stress, lower blood pressure, and improve heart rate variability contributes to a healthier cardiovascular system.

One of the pivotal aspects of meditation is activating the parasympathetic nervous system, often called the "rest and digest" system. This activation induces a state of relaxation, slowing down the heart rate and dilating blood vessels. As a result, blood pressure decreases, reducing the strain on the heart and the risk of heart disease. This isn't just an esoteric concept; it's a scientifically proven benefit of meditation for heart health.

The Mind-Body Symphony

Meditation isn't merely a mental exercise; it's a profound exploration of the mind-body connection. It's a journey where science and spirituality converge, revealing that the mystical experiences of meditation have tangible, scientifically measurable effects on the body. Your brain rewires itself, your neurotransmitters dance with joy, your immune system harmonizes, and your heart beats in rhythmic balance.

As you delve deeper into the world of meditation, you're not just embarking on a spiritual quest; you're also embracing a scientifically validated path to well-being. The ancient wisdom of meditation is beautifully intertwined with the wonders of modern science, showing us that the mind-body connection is a bridge that can lead to a healthier, happier, and more harmonious life. It's a journey that's as fascinating as it is transformational, and it invites you to explore the extraordinary potential within your own mind and body.

A Brief History and Overview of Meditation

Meditation, the practice of focusing one's mind and eliminating distractions to achieve mental clarity and emotional balance, has a rich history that spans thousands of years and cultures across the globe. It's a universal human endeavor that transcends the boundaries of religion, philosophy, and science. Here, we'll embark on a journey through time to explore the history and overview of meditation, from its ancient roots to its modern resurgence as a powerful tool for well-being.

Ancient Beginnings

The origins of meditation are shrouded in the mists of time, making it challenging to pinpoint an exact starting point. However, it's believed that meditation has been practiced for over 5,000 years. One of the earliest documented references to meditation can be found in the ancient Indian scriptures known as the Vedas. These texts, dating back to around 1500 BCE, contain descriptions of meditative practices to achieve a deeper understanding of the self and the universe.

In the Indian tradition, the foundational work on meditation is the "Yoga Sutras" by the sage Patanjali, written around 200 BCE. This text outlines the principles of yoga, a system that incorporates meditation to attain spiritual enlightenment and self-realization.

The Spread of Meditation Practices

Meditation didn't remain confined to India. It spread to various regions and evolved in diverse ways. In China, Taoist meditation practices emerged as integral to Taoist philosophy and spiritual development. Chinese traditions, such as Daoism and Confucianism, also incorporated meditation into their teachings.

Meanwhile, Buddhism, which originated in India and traces its roots to the teachings of Siddhartha Gautama (the Buddha) around 500 BCE, placed significant emphasis on meditation. The Buddha himself is said to have achieved enlightenment through meditation under the Bodhi tree. Buddhist meditation practices, like Vipassana and Zen, continue to be widely practiced to this day.

Meditation reached the Middle East, too, where it became a central element of Sufism, the mystical branch of Islam. In Christian mysticism, practices like contemplative prayer and the Desert Fathers' solitude and meditation played an essential role.

Meditation in the Modern World

While meditation has ancient roots, it didn't become widely known in the Western world until the 20th century. In the 1960s and 70s, there was a surge of interest in Eastern philosophy and spirituality, which brought meditation practices to the forefront. This was partly due to figures like the Maharishi Mahesh Yogi and his popularization of Transcendental Meditation.

The scientific community also began to explore meditation's effects on mental and physical health. Researchers such as Herbert Benson and Jon Kabat-Zinn helped pioneer the field of mindfulness meditation and its applications in stress reduction and overall well-being. Once considered esoteric, meditation practices began to find their way into mainstream psychology and healthcare.

Today, meditation is widely practiced around the world and has taken on a variety of forms. Mindfulness meditation, rooted in Buddhist traditions, has been particularly influential in the West. It involves focusing on the present moment, observing thoughts and emotions without judgment, and promoting self-awareness.

Overview of Meditation Techniques

Meditation is not a one-size-fits-all practice. It encompasses a wide range of techniques, each with its own unique approach and goals. Here are some of the most well-known meditation techniques:

Mindfulness Meditation: This practice involves focusing on the present moment, observing thoughts and sensations without judgment. It's often used for stress reduction and emotional well-being.

Transcendental Meditation: TM involves repeating a specific mantra to reach a state of "restful awareness." It's known for its simplicity and ease of practice.

Loving-Kindness Meditation (Metta): Metta meditation focuses on cultivating compassion and love for oneself and others. It's intended to foster kindness and goodwill.

Vipassana Meditation: An ancient Buddhist practice, Vipassana involves observing the body and mind with insight to gain a deeper understanding of one's experiences and develop wisdom.

Zen Meditation (Zazen): Zen emphasizes seated meditation, often in a group setting. Practitioners focus on the breath and maintain a "just sitting" state of mind.

Guided Visualization: In this form of meditation, a guide leads participants through a mental journey, often with a specific purpose, such as relaxation or personal growth.

Yoga and Movement Meditation: Practices like Tai Chi and Qigong incorporate movement into meditation, promoting physical and mental well-being.

Chakra Meditation: Rooted in Hindu and yogic traditions, chakra meditation focuses on balancing the body's energy centers (chakras) for holistic health.

Mantra Meditation: This involves repeating a word, phrase, or sound (mantra) to focus the mind and induce a state of deep concentration.

Benefits of Meditation

The science of meditation has unveiled a wealth of benefits for mental, emotional, and physical well-being. Research has shown that meditation can reduce stress, anxiety, and depression, enhance concentration and creativity, and even improve the immune system's function. Regular meditation has been associated with increased emotional resilience, heightened self-awareness, and a greater sense of inner peace and calm.

In the fast-paced digital age, meditation has become a powerful antidote to the stress and distractions that often permeate our lives. It's a timeless practice that continues to evolve and adapt to the changing needs of modern society. Meditation's enduring appeal lies in its ability to unlock the potential within each of us, providing a path to self-discovery, emotional balance, and a deeper connection to the world around us.

As you delve into meditation, you'll discover that it's not just a practice; it's a profound journey of self-exploration and self-care. Meditation offers a timeless, scientifically grounded path to enriching your life and nurturing your inner world, whether you seek a moment of tranquillity, a refuge from the chaos of daily life, or a pathway to personal growth and well-being.

The Science Behind Meditation: Illuminating the Mind-Body Connection

Meditation, once relegated to the realms of mysticism and spirituality, has entered modern science's spotlight. Researchers have embarked on a journey to unravel the intricate tapestry of the mind and body's response to meditation in the last few decades. What they've discovered is nothing short of astonishing—a cascade of physiological, neurological, and psychological changes illuminating this ancient practice's profound impact on our well-being. Let's delve into the captivating science behind meditation and explore its transformative power.

The Brain's Symphony

The brain, that enigmatic command center of our bodies, plays a pivotal role in the science of meditation. With the advent of neuroimaging techniques such as fMRI (functional magnetic resonance imaging) and EEG (electroencephalography), scientists have been able to peer into the brain's inner workings as individuals meditate. What they've observed is a fascinating transformation in brain activity.

One of the key areas meditation affects is the prefrontal cortex, often referred to as the brain's "CEO." This region is responsible for executive functions like decision-making, focus, and emotional regulation. Through regular meditation, the prefrontal cortex becomes more finely tuned. This results in improved attention, emotional stability, and cognitive performance. These changes reflect the plasticity of the brain, which adapts and rewires itself in response to the practice of meditation.

Another area of interest is the amygdala, the brain's emotional center. Meditation has been shown to reduce the activity of the amygdala, which translates to a decreased response to stress and emotional reactivity. This is a remarkable finding, as it suggests that meditation can help us remain calm in the face of life's daily challenges. In essence, it equips us with greater emotional resilience.

Furthermore, meditation can increase gray matter density in regions associated with memory and learning, such as the hippocampus. This provides scientific validation for the anecdotal evidence that meditation enhances cognitive function. In essence, regular meditation helps you become more emotionally balanced and mentally sharper.

The Neurochemical Dance

Inside the brain, a symphony of neurotransmitters orchestrates our moods and emotions. Dopamine, serotonin, and endorphins, among others, play a crucial role in determining our feelings of happiness and well-being. The science behind meditation reveals that it can act as a conductor, increasing the production of these "feel-good" chemicals.

Dopamine, often referred to as the "reward neurotransmitter," is responsible for motivation and pleasure. Meditation can boost dopamine levels, leading to an enhanced sense of well-being. Serotonin, a neurotransmitter linked to mood regulation, also sees an increase during meditation, providing a natural way to prevent and manage depression. Meanwhile, releasing endorphins during meditation creates a sense of euphoria, acting as a natural painkiller and mood enhancer.

This neurochemical orchestra is pivotal in enhancing our mental and emotional states. The evidence suggests that meditation isn't merely a mental exercise; it profoundly impacts our brain chemistry, helping us cultivate a sense of happiness and well-being.

The Immune System's Balance

The connection between the mind and the body is not just about mental well-being. It extends to our physical health as well. Our mental state profoundly influences the immune system, our body's defence against illnesses and diseases. Chronic stress weakens the immune system, leaving us vulnerable to infections and diseases. With its ability to reduce stress and inflammation, meditation acts as a soothing balm for our immune system.

Research has shown that meditation can influence the expression of genes related to inflammation. Chronic inflammation is at the root of numerous chronic diseases, including heart disease and cancer. By calming the body's stress response, meditation helps in quelling the fires of inflammation. It's not a mystical claim; it's grounded in the scientific understanding of the intricate interplay between the mind and the immune system.

The Heart of the Matter

In a world where cardiovascular diseases are a leading cause of mortality, the impact of meditation on heart health is especially significant. Meditation's ability to reduce stress, lower blood pressure, and improve heart rate variability contributes to a healthier cardiovascular system.

One of the pivotal aspects of meditation is activating the parasympathetic nervous system, often called the "rest and digest" system. This activation induces relaxation, slowing heart rate and dilating blood vessels. As a result, blood pressure decreases, reducing the strain on the heart and the risk of heart disease. This isn't just an esoteric concept; it's a scientifically proven benefit of meditation for heart health.

The Psychological Landscape

Meditation doesn't just work its magic on our biology; it's a transformative force in psychology and mental health. Studies have demonstrated that meditation can reduce stress, anxiety, and depression. It's a powerful tool for emotional well-being, promoting a sense of inner peace and balance.

One of the foundational concepts in the science of meditation is the "relaxation response." The physiological and psychological shift occurs during meditation, characterised by decreased heart rate, breathing rate, and muscle tension. The relaxation response counters the "fight or flight" response triggered by stress, helping us return to equilibrium.

Meditation cultivates self-awareness and mindfulness, enabling us to observe our thoughts and emotions without judgment. This non-reactive, observant stance is associated with reduced symptoms of anxiety and depression. It's as if meditation equips us with psychological tools to navigate the complex landscape of our thoughts and feelings.

The Confluence of Science and Spirituality

With its revelations about the mind and body's response to this practice, the science of meditation brings to light a confluence of ancient wisdom and modern understanding. It bridges the gap between the mystical meditation experiences and the tangible, scientifically measurable effects on our bodies and minds.

Meditation's appeal lies in its historical significance and its potential to enrich our lives and nurture our inner worlds. It's a practice that continues to evolve and adapt to the changing needs of modern society. Meditation is not merely a mental exercise; it's a journey of self-discovery and self-care, unlocking the potential within each of us and offering a timeless, scientifically grounded path to enriching our lives and nurturing our well-being. The science behind meditation invites us to explore this profound practice with a newfound sense of wonder and appreciation for its transformative power.

Neuroplasticity: Rewiring the Brain

One of the most captivating aspects of meditation from a scientific perspective is its profound impact on brain plasticity, the brain's ability to reorganise and rewire itself. Neuroplasticity is the brain's remarkable capacity to adapt and change in response to experiences, and meditation is a prime example of how this process can be harnessed for personal growth.

Research has demonstrated that regular meditation can promote neuroplasticity by strengthening connections between brain regions responsible for memory, learning, and emotional regulation. For example, studies on mindfulness meditation have shown an increase in gray matter density in the hippocampus, the region linked to memory and learning. This finding suggests that meditation can enhance cognitive abilities and even potentially slow down age-related brain decline.

Moreover, meditation has been found to impact the structure and function of the amygdala, the brain's emotional center. In individuals who practice meditation regularly, the amygdala appears less activated during stressful situations, leading to lower emotional reactivity and a greater capacity to remain calm under pressure.

Mindfulness and Stress Reduction

One of the most widely studied forms of meditation is mindfulness meditation, which encourages focused attention on the present moment. Scientific research has provided evidence supporting its efficacy in reducing stress and its associated health risks.

Stress, while a natural response to perceived threats, becomes problematic when it becomes chronic. Chronic stress can lead to a host of health issues, including high blood pressure, weakened immune function, and increased inflammation. Mindfulness meditation is an antidote to chronic stress by promoting relaxation and reducing the body's production of stress hormones like cortisol.

Studies have shown that regular mindfulness meditation can decrease perceived stress, lower blood pressure, and improve the body's ability to cope with stressors. The practice also enhances emotional regulation and self-awareness, making individuals less susceptible to stress-induced emotional responses.

Emotional Well-Being and Mental Health

In a world where mental health issues like anxiety and depression are on the rise, the role of meditation in promoting emotional well-being is of significant interest. Research has uncovered meditation's potential to alleviate the symptoms of various mental health conditions.

Mindfulness-based approaches, such as Mindfulness-Based Stress Reduction (MBSR) and Mindfulness-Based Cognitive Therapy (MBCT), have been used to help individuals manage depression and prevent recurrent episodes. These programs incorporate mindfulness meditation techniques to encourage non-judgmental awareness of thoughts and emotions, enabling individuals to respond more adaptively to their own psychological challenges.

Furthermore, meditation's impact on anxiety disorders has been extensively studied. The practice can reduce symptoms of generalized anxiety disorder and social anxiety disorder by enhancing emotional regulation, decreasing the activation of the amygdala, and improving overall psychological well-being.

Immune System Boost

The relationship between the mind and the body becomes even more apparent when considering the immune system's response to meditation. Chronic stress weakens the immune system, making individuals more susceptible to illnesses and infections. Meditation, by promoting relaxation and reducing stress, can enhance immune function.

Recent studies have shown that meditation can profoundly affect gene expression related to inflammation. This means that the practice not only reduces stress-induced inflammation but also has the potential to impact chronic diseases linked to excessive inflammation, such as heart disease, cancer, and autoimmune disorders.

The science behind meditation has unveiled a potent mechanism by which the mind can influence the body's health. Meditation is not merely a mental exercise; it is a practice that has a tangible, transformative impact on our biological systems.

A Path to Greater Well-Being

The science behind meditation, emphasising the mind-body connection, bridges ancient wisdom and modern understanding. It illuminates the path to a healthier, happier, and more harmonious life by demonstrating the measurable benefits of this age-old practice.

As you explore the science of meditation, you'll find that it equips you with a deeper appreciation for the practice and its potential to enrich your life. It explores the profound changes within your brain, the transformative effects on your emotional well-being, and the influence on your physical health. Meditation isn't just a means to relax; it's a powerful tool for nurturing your mental and physical well-being. It offers a scientifically grounded path to unlock your inner potential and cultivate a happier, healthier you.

How Meditation Works on the Brain and Body

Meditation, the ancient practice of self-reflection and mindfulness, has captured the imagination of people across the globe for centuries. Its appeal lies in its promise of mental clarity, emotional balance, and inner peace. Amid our fast-paced, digitally driven world, meditation offers a retreat into stillness, where we can explore the intricate connection between the mind and the body. In this exploration, we unravel how meditation works on the brain and the body, understanding the scientific mechanisms that underlie its profound effects.

The Brain's Remarkable Plasticity

The brain, the intricate command centre of our bodies, takes centre stage in understanding the impact of meditation. This chapter delves into neuroplasticity, the brain's ability to rewire and adapt. We explore the scientific evidence that meditation can reconfigure neural pathways, strengthen brain structures, and ultimately enhance mental clarity and emotional equilibrium.

The Neurochemical Magic of Meditation

A symphony of neurotransmitters—serotonin, dopamine, endorphins—orchestrates our moods and emotions within the brain. This chapter unveils the neurochemical effects of meditation, demonstrating how the practice can act as a conductor, boosting the production of "feel-good" neurotransmitters. It elucidates the mechanisms by which meditation enhances mood, reduces anxiety and depression, and fosters a deep sense of well-being.

Immune System and Meditation

The mind-body connection extends to the immune system, the body's defence against diseases. This chapter delves into the profound impact of meditation on the immune system. Chronic stress can weaken our immunity, making us more susceptible to illnesses. Meditation's ability to reduce stress and inflammation is a soothing balm for the immune system. Scientific research shows that meditation can influence gene expression linked to inflammation, potentially reducing the risk of chronic diseases.

Heartfelt Harmony

Cardiovascular diseases are a leading cause of mortality in the modern world. In this chapter, we explore meditation's role in promoting heart health. By reducing stress, lowering blood pressure, and enhancing heart rate variability, meditation contributes to a healthier cardiovascular system. Activating the parasympathetic nervous system, known as the "rest and digest" system, slows the heart rate and dilates blood vessels, further reducing the risk of heart disease.

Psychology of Meditation

Meditation isn't just about biology; it profoundly impacts psychology and mental health. This chapter investigates how meditation alleviates symptoms of anxiety and depression. It sheds light on how the practice reduces stress, enhances emotional regulation, and fosters self-awareness. Additionally, meditation's "relaxation response" counteracts the stress response, helping individuals return to a state of balance.

The interplay between the mind and body is at the core of meditation's transformative power. This chapter emphasises the importance of recognising the intricate connection between the two. Meditation acts as a bridge, uniting mental and physical well-being. It demonstrates that our mental state can significantly impact our physical health and vice versa, reinforcing the need to nurture the mind-body connection.

Emotional resilience, the ability to withstand and recover from life's challenges, is valuable. This chapter reveals how meditation contributes to emotional resilience by reducing the amygdala activation, the brain's vibrant centre. Lower emotional reactivity and improved self-awareness are vital benefits. Meditation also enhances emotional regulation, empowering individuals to adapt to psychological challenges.

Not all meditation techniques are the same, and each style offers unique approaches and advantages. This chapter delves into various meditation styles, from mindfulness and loving-kindness to transcendental meditation and Zen. It highlights each style's distinct benefits and contributions, shedding light on their specific effects on mental clarity, emotional balance, and overall well-being.

With its scientifically validated benefits, meditation invites us to enrich our lives and nurture well-being. This chapter provides a comprehensive guide for those interested in starting their meditation practice. It offers practical tips on beginning, selecting the right meditation style, and overcoming common challenges that newcomers may face. It's an invitation to embark on a journey of self-discovery and inner peace

Meditation Myths and Misconceptions: Separating Fact from Fiction

Meditation is an age-old practice that has endured through centuries and cultures. It promises mental clarity, emotional balance, and inner peace. However, in the modern world, where information flows rapidly, myths and misconceptions about meditation abound. This chapter debunks some of the most common misunderstandings surrounding meditation, allowing us to separate fact from fiction.

Myth 1: Meditation is Only for Spiritual or Religious People

One of the most prevalent myths is that meditation is exclusively a religious or spiritual practice. While it does have deep roots in various spiritual traditions, meditation has also evolved as a secular practice for improving mental and emotional well-being. It's accessible to people from all walks of life, irrespective of their religious or spiritual beliefs.

Myth 2: You Need to Clear Your Mind Completely

A widespread misconception is that you must completely clear your mind of thoughts during meditation. In reality, it's pretty challenging to silence the mind entirely. Meditation is not about emptying the mind but observing thoughts without attachment and returning your focus to a chosen point of attention, such as the breath. It's a practice of cultivating mindfulness, not thought suppression.

Myth 3: Meditation Requires a Lot of Time

Many people believe that meditation demands long hours of practice each day. While some individuals dedicate extensive time to meditation, it's not a strict requirement. Even brief, regular sessions of just a few minutes can yield significant benefits. Consistency is more important than duration, and meditation can easily be incorporated into a busy daily schedule.

Myth 4: Meditation Is a Quick Fix for All Problems

Meditation is a powerful tool for mental and emotional well-being, but it's not a magic wand that instantly solves all life's problems. It's a practice that takes time and commitment to yield its full benefits. While it can alleviate stress, anxiety, and depression, it may not replace the need for medical or therapeutic interventions in some cases.

Myth 5: You Must Sit Cross-Legged on the Floor to Meditate

The image of a person sitting cross-legged on the floor while meditating is common, but it's not the only way to practice. Meditation can be done in various postures, including sitting on a chair, lying down, or walking. The key is finding a comfortable and sustainable position for you.

Myth 6: You Need to Be in a Completely Silent Space

While a quiet environment can be conducive to meditation, it's not always necessary. Meditation can be practised in any setting, even amid noise and distractions. Learning to remain focused in less-than-ideal conditions can strengthen your meditation practice and help you carry mindfulness into everyday life.

Myth 7: Meditation is Escapism

Some people perceive meditation as a form of escapism, a way to avoid dealing with life's challenges. In reality, meditation is about cultivating awareness and presence. It equips you with the mental tools to face life's challenges with resilience and clarity. It's not an escape from reality but a deeper engagement with it.

Myth 8: You Need to Be "Good" at Meditation

There's a common misconception that you must be naturally "good" at meditation to benefit from it. In truth, meditation is a skill that anyone can develop over time. It's not about being good or bad; it's about the practice itself and the progress you make regarding self-awareness and inner peace.

Myth 9: Meditation Is Only About Relaxation

While relaxation is one of the outcomes of meditation, it's not the sole purpose. Meditation can be used for various goals, including enhancing focus, improving emotional regulation, and gaining insight into your thoughts and behaviors. It's a versatile practice with a broad range of applications.

Myth 10: Meditation Is a Loneliness Practice

Meditation is often thought of as a solitary practice. While many meditate alone, it can also be done in a group setting. Group meditation can provide a sense of community and shared energy, enhancing the experience for some practitioners. Meditation can be both a personal and a collective journey.

By dispelling these myths and misconceptions, we better understand meditation's nature and potential. It's a versatile, accessible practice tailored to individual needs and preferences, making it a valuable tool for enhancing mental and emotional well-being.

Tailored Meditation Techniques for Modern Life: Navigating Stress, Anxiety, and Burnout in the Digital Age

In the whirlwind of modern life, where stress, anxiety, and burnout have become commonplace, meditation stands as an oasis of tranquility and self-discovery. This chapter is a comprehensive guide to tailored meditation techniques for modern life, addressing the unique challenges of the digital age and providing a roadmap to achieving mental clarity, emotional balance, and inner peace. As we delve into the multifaceted world of meditation, we'll explore various techniques designed to fit the demands and complexities of contemporary living.

Meditation in the Digital Age

The digital age, characterized by information overload, constant connectivity, and the pressures of a fast-paced lifestyle, presents unique challenges to mental and emotional well-being. This chapter'll explore how tailored meditation techniques can serve as a powerful antidote to the stresses and distractions that permeate our modern lives. We'll also discuss the evolution of meditation practices in response to the changing landscape of the digital age.

Mindfulness Meditation in the Modern World

Mindfulness meditation, rooted in ancient Buddhist traditions, has found renewed relevance in the digital age. We'll delve into the core principles of mindfulness meditation, exploring how it encourages us to focus on the present moment, observe thoughts without judgment, and enhance self-awareness. We'll also discuss its relevance in the modern world.

Techniques for Practicing Mindfulness in a Digital World

Practising mindfulness amidst the digital distractions of our daily lives can be challenging. This section'll explore practical techniques for integrating mindfulness into our digital routines. We'll discuss strategies for managing smartphone and social media usage and using mindfulness to enhance our focus and presence during screen time.

Mindfulness-Based Stress Reduction (MBSR) for the Digital Age

Mindfulness-Based Stress Reduction (MBSR), developed by Dr. Jon Kabat-Zinn, has gained recognition for its efficacy in reducing stress and anxiety. We'll explore how MBSR adapts to the challenges of the digital age and discuss its structured program for cultivating mindfulness in daily life.

Understanding Modern Stressors

In today's fast-paced world, stress manifests in various ways. This section will examine the unique stressors of the digital age, including information overload, work-related stress, and the constant need for connectivity. We'll uncover how tailored meditation techniques can address these modern challenges.

The Science of Stress Reduction through Meditation

Science has given us a deep understanding of how meditation can reduce stress. We'll explore the physiological and psychological mechanisms by which meditation counteracts the effects of stress, promoting relaxation, emotional regulation, and enhanced resilience in the face of modern stressors.

Progressive Muscle Relaxation and Guided Visualization

Progressive muscle relaxation and guided visualization are powerful techniques for stress reduction. We'll delve into how these practices work and how they can be adapted to address modern stressors. We'll also provide step-by-step guidance for incorporating them into your daily routine.

The Rise of Anxiety in the Digital Age

Anxiety disorders are on the rise in the digital age, affecting millions of individuals. This section will examine the factors contributing to this increase, including the pressure of constant connectivity, social media comparisons, and information overload.

Tailored Techniques for Managing Anxiety

Tailored meditation techniques for anxiety management offer practical tools to soothe the anxious mind. We'll explore methods such as diaphragmatic breathing, body scan meditation, and loving-kindness meditation, discussing how they can alleviate anxiety symptoms in the digital age.

The Role of Mindful Self-Compassion in Anxiety Reduction

Self-compassion is a vital component of managing anxiety. We'll discuss the concept of mindful self-compassion and explore how meditation practices, such as Metta (loving-kindness) meditation and self-compassion meditation, can help individuals navigate anxiety while promoting self-care and emotional well-being.

Meditation for Digital Detox and Reconnect

Digital detox, or the intentional reduction of screen time and technology use, has become essential for mental and emotional well-being. We'll examine the reasons behind the need for a digital detox in the digital age and its potential benefits.

Techniques for Digital Detox and Reconnection

This section will provide a range of tailored meditation techniques for digital detox and reconnection. We'll explore practices encouraging individuals to unplug, such as nature meditation, technology-free zones, and mindful breathing outdoors. We'll also discuss how these practices can help individuals reconnect with themselves and the world around them.

Bringing Mindfulness to Technology Use

Rather than seeing technology as the enemy, we can approach it mindfully. We'll explore how individuals can bring mindfulness to their technology use, fostering a healthier relationship with digital devices while maintaining presence and awareness.

Meditation for Burnout Prevention and Recovery

Burnout, characterised by emotional exhaustion, depersonalisation, and reduced personal accomplishment, is a growing concern in the digital age. We'll examine the unique contributors to burnout in modern life, including the blurring of work-life boundaries and constant connectivity.

Techniques for Preventing and Recovering from Burnout

Tailored meditation techniques for burnout prevention and recovery offer a path to resilience and self-care. We'll explore practices such as mindfulness-based burnout prevention, compassion-focused meditation, and self-reflective journaling, providing tools to address the specific challenges of burnout in the digital age.

Creating Work-Life Balance with Meditation

Achieving work-life balance in the digital age is a significant challenge. We'll discuss how meditation can be a powerful tool for creating and maintaining this balance, helping individuals disconnect from work, establish boundaries, and prioritise self-care.

Mindfulness Meditation: Staying Present in a Fast-Paced World

In today's fast-paced, digitally driven world, finding a moment of tranquillity and self-reflection can seem like an elusive goal. The constant influx of information, the pressure to multitask, and the demands of modern life can leave individuals feeling overwhelmed and disconnected from the present moment. Amidst this chaos, mindfulness meditation emerges as a lifeline—enabling individuals to ground themselves in the here and now, fostering mental clarity, emotional balance, and inner peace. In this comprehensive exploration, we will delve deep into mindfulness meditation, elucidating its essence, scientific underpinnings, and practical techniques to stay present in a fast-paced world.

The Essence of Mindfulness Meditation

The journey into the world of mindfulness meditation begins with an exploration of its essence. At its core, mindfulness is a practice that invites individuals to cultivate a heightened awareness of the present moment. This awareness extends to thoughts, sensations, and emotions, and it unfolds without judgment or attachment.

Mindfulness meditation is about observing the ever-flowing stream of consciousness without trying to alter it, judge it, or hold onto it. It's an invitation to immerse oneself in the present, allowing the past and future to recede into the background.

The concept of mindfulness finds its roots in ancient Buddhist traditions, where it is referred to as "sati." However, its relevance and applicability extend far beyond its spiritual origins. Mindfulness has found a place in the modern world, offering solace amid the chaos. It's a practice that can be embraced by individuals of all backgrounds, irrespective of their religious or spiritual beliefs. The heart of mindfulness meditation is about becoming more fully awake to the richness of each moment, which is a timeless and universal aspiration.

Cultivating Mindfulness

Mindfulness meditation is a journey that begins with the cultivation of mindfulness itself. At its essence, mindfulness is about paying deliberate attention to the present moment. This may seem deceptively simple, but it's a transformative undertaking in practice. It involves honing our ability to be fully present, to witness the unfolding of our inner and outer worlds with unbroken attentiveness.

In mindfulness, the breath often serves as an anchor. The point of focus allows individuals to tether themselves to the present moment. Observing the breath as it rises and falls can be a refuge from the ongoing thoughts and distractions. This section will delve into mindful breathing, offering insights on using the breath as a consistent point of connection to the present. Techniques for mindful breathing, such as counting breaths or observing the sensations of the breath, provide a foundation for developing mindfulness.

Breath as the Anchor

The breath's role as an anchor in mindfulness meditation is significant. It is a constant, ever-present aspect of our existence, offering a tangible and accessible point of focus. The act of breathing, which is typically automatic and involuntary, becomes a deliberate and conscious practice in mindfulness. By paying attention to the breath, individuals learn to cultivate an acute awareness of the present moment.

Practicing mindful breathing involves observing the breath without attempting to change or control it. This practice encourages individuals to witness the breath as it naturally occurs, with an attitude of openness and non-judgment. By anchoring one's attention to the breath, individuals can return to the present moment whenever they find themselves lost in thought or preoccupied with worries.

The Mindful Body Scan

The mindful body scan is another powerful technique used in mindfulness meditation. This practice involves systematically directing one's attention to different parts of the body, from head to toe, in a deliberate and methodical manner. The objective is to develop a heightened awareness of physical sensations, tension, or discomfort that may be present in the body.

During a mindful body scan, individuals are encouraged to explore their bodies with a sense of curiosity and acceptance. The practice often starts at the crown of the head and gradually moves down to the toes. With each segment of the body, the focus is on observing any sensations, tightness, or areas of discomfort. The body scan is a profound practice for grounding oneself in the physical sensations of the present moment, promoting relaxation, and enhancing overall well-being.

Neuroplasticity and Mindfulness

The transformative power of mindfulness meditation finds its scientific validation in the concept of neuroplasticity—the brain's ability to reorganize and adapt. This section explores how mindfulness meditation shapes the brain's structure and function, highlighting the remarkable capacity of the mind to change.

Research has demonstrated that regular mindfulness meditation can lead to an increase in gray matter density in certain brain regions, such as the hippocampus. This region is associated with memory and learning, and its expansion suggests that mindfulness can enhance cognitive abilities. Additionally, the practice influences the amygdala, the brain's emotional center. In individuals who meditate regularly, the amygdala appears to be less activated during stressful situations, leading to lower emotional reactivity and greater calm under pressure.

The concept of neuroplasticity implies that our mental habits and practices can have a tangible effect on our brain structure. Mindfulness meditation stands as a powerful tool for harnessing this inherent capacity, molding the brain in ways that promote mental clarity, emotional balance, and well-being.

Mindfulness-Based Stress Reduction

Mindfulness-Based Stress Reduction (MBSR), developed by Dr. Jon Kabat-Zinn, is a structured program that has garnered recognition for its efficacy in reducing stress, anxiety, and enhancing overall well-being. In this section, we explore the foundations of MBSR and its adaptability to the challenges of the digital age.

MBSR is built on the principles of mindfulness, incorporating practices such as mindful breathing, body scan meditation, and mindful yoga. The program typically spans eight weeks and offers a structured approach to cultivating mindfulness in everyday life. MBSR teaches participants to observe their thoughts and emotions without attachment or judgment, fostering self-awareness and emotional regulation.

The evidence-based nature of MBSR has made it an appealing choice for individuals seeking stress reduction in the modern world. Research has demonstrated its effectiveness in reducing symptoms of anxiety, depression, and improving overall mental well-being. The program offers a roadmap to integrating mindfulness into daily routines and managing the stressors of contemporary living.

Mindfulness and Emotional Regulation

Emotional regulation is a central aspect of well-being, and mindfulness meditation exerts a profound influence in this domain. This section explores the scientific mechanisms by which mindfulness reduces emotional reactivity and enhances self-awareness.

The amygdala, a small, almond-shaped structure deep within the brain, plays a crucial role in emotional processing. It is responsible for detecting threats and initiating the body's stress response. In individuals who regularly practice mindfulness, the amygdala appears to be less activated during emotionally charged situations. This dampened response leads to reduced emotional reactivity and a greater sense of calm during stressful moments.

Moreover, mindfulness enhances self-awareness, allowing individuals to recognize their emotions without becoming overwhelmed by them. This heightened self-awareness fosters a sense of emotional regulation, empowering individuals to respond adaptively to challenging situations. Mindfulness also encourages the development of a "pause and choose" response rather than an automatic "react and regret" reaction.

Integrating Mindfulness into Digital Life

The digital age brings with it a host of distractions, from the constant pinging of smartphones to the allure of social media and the ceaseless demands of digital communication. This section delves into practical techniques for integrating mindfulness into daily digital life.

Mindful smartphone usage is a pivotal consideration. With the omnipresence of smartphones, the compulsion to check messages, scroll through social media, and respond to notifications can be incessant. Mindfulness offers an alternative, a means to approach smartphone usage with deliberate presence. Techniques for mindful smartphone usage include setting specific times for checking messages, establishing technology-free zones, and learning to pause and breathe before reacting to notifications.

Mindful Work and Productivity

The workplace is often a hotbed of stress, multitasking, and mental clutter. Mindfulness can be an invaluable tool for improving work-related productivity and well-being. In this section, we explore how the practice of mindfulness can enhance focus, reduce stress, and foster a sense of presence during tasks.

Mindfulness at work involves bringing one's full attention to the task at hand. It encourages individuals to focus on a single task rather than attempting to juggle multiple tasks simultaneously. This approach, known as "single-tasking," has been shown to enhance productivity and reduce the cognitive load associated with multitasking.

Mindful breaks and pauses during the workday are also crucial for recharging and maintaining presence. Short, mindful breathing exercises or mini-meditations can provide a respite from the demands of work, allowing individuals to return to their tasks with renewed focus and clarity.

Mindfulness for Stress Reduction

In the digital age, stress can manifest in various forms, including information overload, work-related pressures, and the incessant demands of the digital world. This section explores specific mindfulness techniques for reducing the stress associated with these modern challenges.

Mindful breathing, as previously mentioned, is a fundamental practice for reducing stress. This technique involves returning one's focus to the breath, observing it with an attitude of curiosity and openness. It acts as a reset button, allowing individuals to release tension and return to the present moment.

Mini-meditations or micro-moments of mindfulness can be seamlessly integrated into daily routines. These brief, focused practices can help individuals alleviate stress and regain mental clarity. For example, individuals can engage in mindful breathing exercises while waiting in line, during a short break, or while stuck in traffic.

In the midst of the digital age's complexities, mindfulness serves as an anchor, a means of staying present amidst the chaos. The practice of mindfulness has been scientifically validated, revealing its profound impact on the brain, emotional regulation, and overall well-being.

The journey of mindfulness is a deeply personal one. It encourages individuals to embark on their own path, exploring the practice and uncovering its relevance to their lives. It is a practice that can be integrated into daily routines, offering respite from the relentless pace of modern life. Ultimately, mindfulness is an invitation to immerse oneself in the richness of each moment, to awaken to the present, and to navigate the complexities of the digital age with greater clarity, resilience, and inner peace.

Breathing Techniques: Calming the Anxious Mind

Amid the hustle and bustle of our fast-paced lives, anxiety has become a prevalent issue. The constant demands, digital distractions, and the pace of modern life can leave individuals feeling overwhelmed and anxious. Breathing techniques, rooted in ancient wisdom and supported by contemporary science, provide a potent antidote to this pervasive problem. In this comprehensive exploration, we'll delve into the world of breathing techniques, understanding their significance, and discovering practical methods for calming the anxious mind.

The Breath as a Gateway to Calmness

The act of breathing is one of the most fundamental and automatic processes of life. It is the very essence of our existence, an ever-present companion accompanying us from birth to the end of life. The remarkable aspect of breathing is that, despite its automatic nature, it can also be consciously controlled. This duality forms the basis of the profound effect that breathing techniques have on our mental and emotional well-being.

Breathing is intimately linked to our state of mind. In moments of calm, the breath flows effortlessly and harmoniously. In times of stress and anxiety, the breath becomes shallow and rapid, reflecting our inner turmoil. The understanding of this connection between the breath and the mind forms the foundation of breathing techniques for calming the anxious mind.

The Science of Breathing

The connection between the breath and the body is a powerful one. When we become anxious, our sympathetic nervous system is activated, initiating the "fight or flight" response. This response triggers shallow, rapid breathing, preparing the body to respond to a perceived threat.

On the other hand, when we breathe slowly and deeply, we activate the parasympathetic nervous system, responsible for the "rest and digest" response. This activates a state of relaxation, reducing heart rate and promoting a sense of calm.

Understanding this connection between the breath and the body provides the scientific rationale for the use of breathing techniques to manage anxiety. By consciously controlling the breath, we can shift our physiological state from one of stress to one of relaxation.

Diaphragmatic Breathing

Diaphragmatic breathing, also known as abdominal or deep breathing, is a fundamental breathing technique for calming the anxious mind. It involves engaging the diaphragm, a large muscle located beneath the lungs, to draw air deep into the lungs. This technique is a stark contrast to shallow chest breathing, which is common in moments of anxiety.

Diaphragmatic breathing triggers the relaxation response in the body. It slows the heart rate, reduces blood pressure, and promotes a sense of calm. This section delves into the mechanics of diaphragmatic breathing and provides guidance on how to practice it effectively. It explores the use of breath awareness, visualizations, and progressive muscle relaxation to enhance the effectiveness of diaphragmatic breathing.

Techniques for Calming the Anxious Mind

In the hustle and bustle of our modern lives, where stress and anxiety often seem to be constant companions, finding moments of calm and tranquillity can be a precious gift. In this chapter, we delve into a variety of techniques designed to help you tame the restless mind and discover the profound benefits of inner peace. "Techniques for Calming the Anxious Mind" offers a practical exploration of methods such as 4-7-8 breathing, box breathing, Alternate Nostril Breathing (Nadi Shodhana), and Mindful Breathing. Whether you're seeking a quick escape from the chaos of daily life or a more sustained practice for lasting serenity, this chapter is your guide to unlocking the power of meditation in our fast-paced, modern world. Embrace these techniques, and embark on a journey towards a calmer, more centered you.

The 4-7-8 Breathing Technique

The 4-7-8 breathing technique is a simple yet potent practice for reducing anxiety and stress. It involves inhaling for a count of four, holding the breath for a count of seven, and exhaling for a count of eight. This extended exhalation triggers the relaxation response and helps calm the anxious mind.

We explore the step-by-step process of the 4-7-8 technique, providing a practical guide on incorporating it into daily routines. Additionally, we discuss its adaptability to various situations, making it a versatile tool for managing anxiety in different contexts.

Box Breathing

Box breathing, also known as square breathing, is a technique that emphasizes symmetry and balance. It involves inhaling, holding the breath, exhaling, and holding the breath again, each for a count of the same duration, typically four seconds. This balanced approach promotes a sense of stability and tranquility.

In this section, we delve into the practice of box breathing, offering insights on maintaining a sense of balance and calm amid anxiety. We explore technique variations, such as the 4-4-4-4 and 5-5-5-5 patterns, to suit individual preferences.

Alternate Nostril Breathing (Nadi Shodhana)

Alternate nostril breathing, a technique derived from yoga, offers a unique approach to calming the anxious mind. It involves using the thumb and forefinger to alternate the closing and opening of nostrils during the breath cycle. This rhythmic practice balances the body's energy flow, promoting relaxation and mental clarity.

We explore the alternate nostril breathing technique, providing a step-by-step guide to mastering it. We also discuss this ancient practice's philosophy and principles, shedding light on its efficacy in managing anxiety.

Mindful Breathing

Mindfulness, a practice that invites individuals to cultivate present-moment awareness, can be seamlessly integrated with breathing techniques. In this section, we explore the concept of mindful breathing, which involves bringing full attention to the breath without judgment or distraction.

Mindful breathing encourages individuals to observe the breath as it naturally occurs, with an attitude of curiosity and openness. We delve into the practice of mindful breathing and its impact on reducing anxiety. Mindful breathing serves as a bridge between the breath and the mind, promoting self-awareness and emotional regulation.

Breath as an Anchor in Mindfulness Meditation

The breath often serves as an anchor in mindfulness meditation. It provides a focal point for individuals to tether themselves to the present moment. This section explores how the breath anchors individuals in the here and now, serving as a refuge from the relentless stream of thoughts and worries.

By using the breath as an anchor, individuals can return to the present moment whenever they find themselves lost in thought or overwhelmed by anxiety. The breath is a constant and accessible point of connection, offering a sense of stability and calm.

Harnessing the Power of the Breath

In the conclusion of this exploration of breathing techniques for calming the anxious mind, it is important to reiterate the profound connection between the breath and mental well-being. The breath is a gateway to calmness and serenity, accessible to us at any moment.

The practice of diaphragmatic breathing, 4-7-8 breathing, box breathing, and alternate nostril breathing offers a diverse array of techniques that can be tailored to individual preferences and situations. When integrated with mindfulness, these techniques become even more potent, fostering self-awareness and emotional regulation.

Breathing techniques provide individuals with a tangible means of managing anxiety and promoting mental and emotional well-being. In the midst of the fast-paced, anxiety-inducing world we live in, these techniques serve as tools of empowerment, offering a path to inner peace and tranquility. Whether practiced in moments of acute anxiety or as a daily ritual for stress prevention, breathing techniques offer a refuge from the storm of the anxious mind.

Body Scan Meditation: Releasing Tension and Stress

In our fast-paced and often stressful lives, the body often bears the brunt of our anxiety and tension. Body scan meditation is a transformative practice that offers respite by promoting deep relaxation and releasing the accumulated stress and tension that the body holds. In this exploration, we'll delve into the world of body scan meditation, understanding its significance, and discovering practical methods for achieving physical and mental well-being through this powerful technique.

The Mind-Body Connection

The human body is an intricate tapestry of sensations, emotions, and experiences. The stresses and anxieties of modern life can cause physical tension to accumulate, resulting in discomfort and pain. Understanding the connection between the mind and the body is the key to comprehending the power of body scan meditation.

When we experience stress and anxiety, the body responds with muscle tension, shallow breathing, and heightened physiological arousal. These physical manifestations of anxiety can, in turn, intensify our mental distress. Body scan meditation recognizes this bidirectional relationship and offers a means of breaking the cycle by systematically guiding individuals to focus on each part of their body, release tension, and attain deep relaxation.

The Essence of Body Scan Meditation

Body scan meditation is a practice rooted in mindfulness and somatic awareness. It invites individuals to turn their attention inward, exploring the body with a sense of gentle curiosity. The practice unfolds by systematically directing one's focus to various parts of the body, starting typically from the toes and moving up to the head.

The essence of body scan meditation is about observing without judgment. It's a practice that encourages individuals to witness physical sensations, discomfort, and tension without attempting to change or resist them. This non-judgmental awareness is a cornerstone of the practice, fostering self-compassion and relaxation.

The practice of body scan meditation is deeply intertwined with the mind-body connection. As individuals move their attention through different parts of the body, they develop an acute awareness of physical sensations. This heightened awareness allows individuals to recognize tension, discomfort, and areas of stress that they might not have been conscious of otherwise.

As the mind identifies these areas of physical tension, the body scan meditation provides a means to release and relax them. By paying attention to the body in a systematic and compassionate manner, individuals can alleviate the physical discomfort that results from stress and anxiety.

The Physiology of Stress and Tension

To comprehend the science behind body scan meditation, it's essential to grasp the physiological underpinnings of stress and tension in the body. When we experience stress or anxiety, the sympathetic nervous system is activated, leading to the "fight or flight" response. This response results in muscle tension, shallow breathing, and other physical manifestations of stress.

The tension that accumulates in the body can lead to discomfort and pain, further exacerbating the experience of stress and anxiety. Understanding the body's physiological response to stress highlights the significance of practices like body scan meditation in promoting relaxation and well-being.

Relaxation Response

The relaxation response, the counterpoint to the "fight or flight" response, is the foundation of body scan meditation. As individuals move their attention through the body during the practice, they encourage the activation of the parasympathetic nervous system, responsible for the "rest and digest" response. This activation leads to a state of relaxation, reducing heart rate, lowering blood pressure, and promoting a sense of calm.

Scientific research has supported the effectiveness of practices like body scan meditation in triggering the relaxation response. Studies have shown that regular practice can lead to a reduction in muscle tension, pain, and the physiological indicators of stress.

Getting Started with Body Scan Meditation

Embarking on a body scan meditation practice doesn't require any special equipment or expertise. It can be performed by anyone, anywhere, and at any time. This section offers a step-by-step guide on getting started with body scan meditation, highlighting the importance of finding a comfortable and quiet space to practice.

We explore techniques for beginning the practice, such as establishing a relaxed posture and setting an intention for the meditation. The chapter provides a basic outline of the practice, typically starting from the toes and moving upward through the body. The guidance emphasizes maintaining an attitude of non-judgment and compassion throughout the practice.

Focusing on Breath and Sensation

Body scan meditation often integrates awareness of breath and physical sensations. This section delves into the role of breath in body scan meditation, highlighting how individuals can use their breath to anchor their awareness to the present moment.

The practice encourages individuals to breathe into areas of tension, allowing the breath to promote relaxation and release discomfort.

Observing physical sensations, such as warmth, tingling, or even discomfort, is another integral aspect of body scan meditation. This section offers insights into how to bring mindful attention to these sensations, enhancing the depth of the practice.

The Role of Visualization in Body Scan Meditation

Visualization can play a significant role in body scan meditation. By mentally envisioning the breath as a soothing, healing energy, individuals can enhance the practice's effectiveness. This section provides guidance on incorporating visualization techniques into body scan meditation, offering tools to deepen the relaxation response and release tension.

Visualization techniques can include imagining a warm, glowing light moving through the body, melting away tension and promoting a profound sense of relaxation. Additionally, visualizing physical sensations as fluid and dynamic can aid in the release of stress and discomfort.

Finding Relief and Well-Being

In the fast-paced, often stressful world we inhabit, practices like body scan meditation provide a sanctuary for the body and the mind. The mind-body connection is a powerful force, and body scan meditation acknowledges and utilizes this connection to foster deep relaxation and physical well-being.

By systematically guiding individuals to focus on each part of their body, release tension, and attain deep relaxation, body scan meditation offers a path to tranquility and inner peace. The science behind the practice confirms its effectiveness in promoting the relaxation response and reducing the physical manifestations of stress.

In the conclusion of this exploration, it is important to emphasize the transformative potential of body scan meditation. This practice serves as a potent tool for releasing tension, alleviating stress, and enhancing physical and mental well-being. Whether incorporated into daily routines or used as a respite in moments of acute stress, body scan meditation offers a sanctuary of relief and a path to a more relaxed and balanced life.

Walking Meditation: Finding Peace in Motion

In our ever-accelerating world, the act of walking often becomes a rush from one place to another. We hurry through our days, often missing the simple pleasures and moments of tranquility that walking can provide. Walking meditation, rooted in mindfulness and ancient traditions, offers a profound way to find peace in motion. In this exploration, we'll delve into the world of walking meditation, understanding its significance, and discovering practical methods for embracing mindfulness and serenity while on the move.

The Lost Art of Walking

Walking is a universal activity, one that we engage in daily without much thought. Yet, in our quest for efficiency and productivity, we often overlook the transformative potential of this simple act. The introduction of walking meditation serves as a gentle reminder that even the most mundane activities can become vehicles for profound self-awareness and tranquility.

Walking meditation is a practice that encourages individuals to cultivate mindfulness and awareness as they walk. It can be performed anywhere, whether on a quiet forest path or in the midst of a bustling city. The essence of walking meditation is about being fully present in each step, observing the sensations, and embracing the beauty of the journey rather than the destination.

The Essence of Walking Meditation

Walking meditation is an extension of traditional seated meditation practices. It invites individuals to bring their full attention to the act of walking, embracing each step with mindfulness and presence. The essence of walking meditation is about being fully engaged in the experience, releasing thoughts of the past or future, and grounding oneself in the present moment.

This section explores the fundamental principles of walking meditation, emphasizing the importance of walking slowly and deliberately. The practice encourages individuals to notice the sensations of each step, the feeling of contact with the earth, and the rhythm of their breath as they walk. The practice fosters self-awareness and calmness in motion.

The Mindfulness of Each Step

Mindfulness is at the heart of walking meditation. This practice encourages individuals to become aware of each step they take, recognizing the sensations and experiences associated with walking. The act of paying attention to each step, without judgment or attachment, allows individuals to become deeply attuned to their bodies and the environment.

We explore techniques for developing mindfulness in each step, emphasizing the use of breath awareness as a tool for staying present. The guidance encourages individuals to release the rush and distractions of the mind, finding peace in the simplicity of moving one step at a time.

Embracing the Senses

Walking meditation is a sensory experience. This section delves into the practice of embracing the senses as individuals walk. It encourages individuals to observe the sights, sounds, and sensations of the environment, fostering a heightened state of awareness and presence.

The guidance emphasizes the importance of noticing the world around us—the feel of the breeze, the chirping of birds, the rustling of leaves. By engaging the senses in this way, walking meditation becomes a means of connecting with the world, offering a sense of unity and oneness with nature and surroundings.

The Psychology of Mindful Movement

The practice of walking meditation is rooted in the psychology of mindful movement. This section explores the profound impact that walking meditation can have on the mind and emotional well-being. Studies have shown that mindful movement practices like walking meditation can reduce symptoms of anxiety, depression, and stress.

The practice of walking meditation encourages the activation of the parasympathetic nervous system, responsible for the "rest and digest" response. This activation leads to a state of relaxation, reduced heart rate, and a sense of calm. We delve into the scientific mechanisms behind this process, highlighting the potential of walking meditation to enhance emotional regulation.

Walking Meditation and Improved Focus

The act of walking meditation has also been associated with improved focus and concentration. It is not merely a physical practice; it also engages the mind, requiring sustained attention to each step and breath. This section explores the science behind how walking meditation can enhance cognitive function.

Studies have shown that walking meditation can lead to increased attention and memory. The practice encourages individuals to develop a deeper connection to the present moment, freeing the mind from the distractions and stress of daily life.

Getting Started with Walking Meditation

The beauty of walking meditation is its accessibility. It doesn't require any special equipment or location. This section offers practical guidance on getting started with walking meditation. It emphasizes the importance of finding a comfortable place to walk, whether it's a quiet park, a garden, or a simple path.

We explore techniques for beginning the practice, including finding a relaxed and natural posture and setting a comfortable walking pace. The guidance encourages individuals to release any expectations or pressures, embracing the practice with an open heart and mind.

Step-by-Step Walking Meditation

Walking meditation often follows a structured sequence. In this section, we offer a step-by-step guide to practicing walking meditation. The practice typically starts with taking a few moments to stand still and become aware of the body's presence. Individuals then begin walking slowly and deliberately, focusing on the sensations of each step.

We explore the role of breath awareness in walking meditation, encouraging individuals to synchronize their breath with their steps. This alignment between breath and movement offers a sense of rhythm and flow, enhancing the mindfulness of each step.

Incorporating Walking Meditation into Daily Life

The practice of walking meditation can be seamlessly integrated into daily life. This section delves into ways of incorporating walking meditation into daily routines. Whether walking from home to work, during a lunch break, or as a prelude to seated meditation, individuals can find moments of serenity and presence through walking.

The guidance emphasizes the adaptability of walking meditation to different settings and timeframes, offering practical tools for embracing mindfulness in motion.

Finding Peace in the Journey

As we conclude this exploration of walking meditation, it is important to highlight the transformative potential of the practice. Walking meditation is a means of finding peace in the journey, rather than fixating on the destination.

The scientific underpinnings of the practice reveal its capacity to reduce stress, enhance emotional regulation, and improve focus. In the midst of a fast-paced and often stressful world, walking meditation serves as a refuge, offering moments of tranquillity and mindfulness in motion.

The conclusion reiterates the simple yet profound truth that walking can be a path to inner peace. Whether used as a standalone practice or an addition to one's mindfulness routine, walking meditation offers a way to find serenity in motion and embrace the beauty of each step on life's journey.

Digital Detox Meditation: Reclaiming Your Time and Attention

In the age of constant connectivity and digital distractions, the need for a "digital detox" has become increasingly urgent. The relentless buzz of notifications, the allure of social media, and the endless stream of information can leave us feeling overwhelmed and disconnected from the present moment. Digital detox meditation offers a path to reclaim your time and attention, fostering mental clarity, emotional balance, and a renewed sense of presence. In this exploration, we'll delve into the world of digital detox meditation, understanding its significance, and discovering practical methods for breaking free from the digital grip.

The Digital Age Dilemma

The digital age has brought us remarkable advances in technology and communication, but it has also introduced new challenges. Our devices, meant to enhance our lives, often dominate them instead. The constant connectivity to smartphones, social media, and a barrage of notifications has led to a growing sense of digital overwhelm.

The introduction of digital detox meditation acknowledges the toll that this constant connectivity can take on our mental and emotional well-being. It offers a means of breaking free from the digital grip, restoring our connection to the present moment, and cultivating mindfulness amidst the digital noise.

Understanding Digital Detox

Digital detox, at its core, is about taking a break from the digital world and reclaiming your time and attention. It involves temporarily disconnecting from digital devices, social media, and the constant barrage of information. The essence of digital detox meditation is to utilize this break as an opportunity to cultivate mindfulness and reconnect with the present moment.

This section explores the fundamental principles of digital detox meditation, emphasizing the importance of setting boundaries and creating a mindful space free from digital distractions. It encourages individuals to embrace the simplicity of life without screens and notifications, fostering a sense of presence and well-being.

Mindfulness in the Digital Age

Mindfulness, the practice of being fully present and non-judgmental, is at the heart of digital detox meditation. In the digital age, it's easy to become entangled in the constant stream of information, reacting to notifications and multitasking. Mindfulness offers an alternative—a path to step back from the digital chaos and regain control of our attention.

We explore the essence of mindfulness in the digital age, highlighting its role in enhancing awareness and emotional regulation. By practicing mindfulness, individuals can develop a sense of presence and a profound connection to the here and now.

The Impact of Digital Overwhelm

The constant exposure to digital devices and information can have a significant impact on our mental and emotional well-being. Research has shown that excessive screen time and digital distractions can lead to increased stress, anxiety, and decreased attention span.

This section delves into the scientific underpinnings of digital overwhelm, highlighting the psychological and physiological effects of constant digital connectivity. Understanding the impact of digital distractions reinforces the significance of practices like digital detox meditation.

The Power of Mindfulness in Detoxing

The practice of mindfulness has been shown to be an effective tool for reducing the impact of digital overwhelm. Studies have demonstrated that mindfulness can reduce symptoms of stress and anxiety, enhance emotional regulation, and improve overall mental well-being.

The section explores the science behind how mindfulness serves as an antidote to digital distractions. It discusses how mindfulness cultivates the ability to focus and regain control over one's attention in the face of digital overload.

Getting Started with Digital Detox Meditation

Digital detox meditation is a practice that can be embarked on by individuals of all backgrounds, regardless of their level of experience with mindfulness. This section offers practical guidance on getting started with digital detox meditation. It emphasizes the importance of creating a mindful space free from digital devices and notifications.

We explore techniques for beginning the practice, including setting clear intentions and boundaries for the detox period. The guidance encourages individuals to inform family and friends about their digital detox, ensuring a supportive environment for the practice.

Disconnecting Mindfully

In the digital detox period, disconnecting from digital devices is essential. This section offers insights on how to disconnect mindfully, emphasizing the importance of being intentional about the process. It encourages individuals to turn off notifications, set specific times for checking emails and messages, and create digital-free zones in their living spaces.

Mindful disconnection involves embracing the simplicity of life without screens and creating a space for presence and reflection. It serves as a foundation for the practice of digital detox meditation.

The Art of Mindful Presence

Digital detox meditation invites individuals to embrace the art of mindful presence. This section explores techniques for developing mindfulness amidst the detox period. It encourages individuals to observe the sensations, sounds, and experiences of the present moment without judgment or distraction.

The practice encourages individuals to explore the beauty of simple activities—such as walking in nature, engaging in mindful breathing, or savoring a meal—while fully immersed in the experience. By cultivating mindfulness, individuals can break free from the digital grip and rediscover the richness of the present moment.

Embracing Mindfulness in the Digital Age

As we conclude this exploration of digital detox meditation, it is essential to reiterate the transformative potential of the practice. In the digital age, digital detox meditation serves as a beacon of hope, offering a respite from the relentless stream of information and a path to greater presence.

The conclusion highlights the importance of digital detox as a means of reclaiming time and attention, fostering mental clarity, emotional balance, and a renewed sense of presence. It is a practice that can be integrated into daily life, offering moments of serenity amidst the digital noise.

Ultimately, digital detox meditation is an invitation to disconnect from the digital world temporarily, to rediscover the joy of the present moment, and to cultivate mindfulness amidst the digital age's challenges. It is a path to reclaiming your time, attention, and well-being in a world filled with digital distractions.

Dealing with Resistance and Distractions in Meditation

Meditation is a transformative practice, offering a sanctuary for the mind to rest and rejuvenate. Yet, even the most seasoned meditators encounter resistance and distractions. In this comprehensive guide, we'll explore the multifaceted nature of resistance and distractions in meditation. We'll delve into realistic distractions, from wandering thoughts to external disruptions, and provide practical strategies for resisting and overcoming them. By understanding the challenges and embracing effective techniques, you can cultivate a more fulfilling and consistent meditation practice.

The Inner Battle of Meditation

Meditation is often portrayed as a serene journey into inner peace. However, anyone who's earnestly tried meditation knows that the path is riddled with challenges. It's not uncommon to encounter resistance and distractions that can disrupt your practice. Understanding these challenges is the first step toward transcending them.

The introduction sets the stage for the exploration of resistance and distractions in meditation. It acknowledges the expectation of finding serenity in meditation and counters it with the reality of inner battles. By embracing the multifaceted nature of meditation, individuals can approach the practice with greater resilience and determination.

The Nature of Resistance in Meditation

Resistance is a common companion in meditation. It often manifests as a reluctance to sit down and meditate or as a constant urge to disengage from the practice. This section delves into the inner resistance that individuals experience in meditation.

We explore the psychological underpinnings of resistance, which can be rooted in discomfort, restlessness, or avoidance of difficult emotions. The guidance offers insights into acknowledging resistance without judgment and developing self-compassion as a means to transcend it. It encourages individuals to view resistance as a natural part of the meditation journey, one that can be confronted with understanding and patience.

The Role of Expectations

Expectations play a significant role in resistance. Individuals often come to meditation with preconceived notions of what the practice should be like, and when it doesn't align with their expectations, resistance arises. This section delves into the influence of expectations in creating resistance.

We discuss the importance of letting go of expectations and approaching meditation with an open mind. The guidance emphasizes that meditation is a unique journey for each individual, and comparing one's experience to others can lead to resistance. By embracing the practice as it unfolds, individuals can diminish the impact of expectations on their meditation.

Realistic Distractions in Meditation

Wandering Thoughts

Wandering thoughts are a pervasive distraction in meditation. The mind is naturally inclined to drift, jumping from one thought to another without invitation. This section explores the nature of wandering thoughts and their impact on meditation.

We discuss the role of the "monkey mind" in causing wandering thoughts and provide insights into the transient nature of thoughts. The guidance offers techniques for working with wandering thoughts, including acknowledging them without judgment, returning to the point of focus, and using anchors like the breath to tether the mind. By understanding the nature of wandering thoughts and learning to navigate them, individuals can minimize their disruptive influence.

External Disruptions

External disruptions are another common challenge in meditation. These can range from noise pollution and sudden interruptions to physical discomfort. This section delves into the impact of external disruptions on meditation and offers strategies for resisting their influence.

We discuss the importance of creating a conducive environment for meditation, including finding a quiet space and using tools like earplugs or ambient music to minimize external distractions. The guidance emphasizes the role of acceptance, teaching individuals to recognize that external disruptions are a natural part of life and can be approached with equanimity. By incorporating these strategies, individuals can maintain focus in the face of external challenges.

Practical Strategies for Resisting Resistance and Distractions

Breath as an Anchor

The breath serves as a powerful anchor in meditation, helping individuals resist distractions and remain present. This section explores the significance of the breath in meditation and offers guidance on using it as a focal point.

We discuss various breath-based techniques, such as mindful breathing and deep diaphragmatic breathing. The guidance provides practical instructions on how to use the breath as an anchor during meditation. By incorporating breath awareness, individuals can cultivate a greater sense of presence and reduce the impact of distractions.

Mindful Observation

Mindful observation is a technique that encourages individuals to approach distractions with curiosity and awareness. This section delves into the practice of mindful observation and its role in dealing with resistance and distractions.

We discuss how individuals can turn their attention to distractions rather than attempting to push them away. By observing distractions mindfully, individuals gain insights into their nature and their potential to disrupt meditation. The guidance emphasizes that by observing distractions without judgment, individuals can diminish their disruptive power and maintain a sense of presence.

Acceptance and Non-Judgment

Acceptance and non-judgment are foundational principles in meditation. This section explores the significance of embracing resistance and distractions without self-criticism.

We discuss the concept of non-judgment, emphasizing that meditation is not about eradicating resistance or distractions but about working with them skillfully. The guidance encourages individuals to adopt an attitude of self-compassion and patience. By recognizing that resistance and distractions are natural aspects of meditation, individuals can resist the temptation to criticize themselves and, instead, cultivate a sense of understanding and kindness.

Cultivating Consistency in Meditation

Establishing a Routine

Consistency is a key factor in overcoming resistance and distractions in meditation. This section explores the importance of establishing a meditation routine and offers insights into creating a sustainable practice.

We discuss the benefits of routine, including how it helps individuals become more attuned to the meditation process and reduces resistance over time. The guidance provides practical strategies for integrating meditation into daily life, such as setting a regular time for practice and creating a dedicated meditation space. By establishing a routine, individuals can make meditation an integral part of their lives and diminish the influence of resistance and distractions.

Patience and Perseverance

Patience and perseverance are invaluable qualities in meditation. This section delves into the role of these qualities in resisting resistance and distractions.

We discuss the necessity of patience when dealing with resistance and distractions, recognizing that progress in meditation often unfolds gradually. The guidance encourages individuals to cultivate perseverance, acknowledging that challenges are an inherent part of the journey. By embracing these qualities, individuals can resist the urge to give up when confronted with resistance and distractions, allowing their meditation practice to flourish.

The Ongoing Journey of Meditation

As we conclude this comprehensive guide on dealing with resistance and distractions in meditation, it's vital to reiterate that meditation is an ongoing journey. It is not about achieving perfection or eliminating all distractions but about cultivating mindfulness and inner awareness.

The conclusion underscores the transformative potential of meditation, emphasizing the benefits of reduced resistance and distractions, including increased focus, emotional regulation, and inner peace. It encourages individuals to approach meditation with an open heart, recognizing that the challenges of resistance and distractions are natural aspects of the practice.

Ultimately, by understanding the multifaceted nature of resistance and distractions in meditation and embracing practical strategies, individuals can deepen their meditation practice and navigate the inner battles with greater skill and resilience.

Building a Consistent Meditation Practice

Meditation is a transformative practice that offers numerous benefits for mental, emotional, and physical well-being. However, for many, building a consistent meditation practice can be challenging. In this comprehensive guide, we'll explore the essential elements and practical strategies for establishing and maintaining a meditation routine. Whether you're a beginner looking to start a practice or someone seeking to rekindle a habit, this guide will provide you with the knowledge and tools needed to build a consistent and rewarding meditation practice.

The Power of Consistency in Meditation

The benefits of meditation are well-documented, from reduced stress and improved focus to enhanced emotional regulation and greater overall well-being. However, to reap these rewards, consistency is key. The introduction highlights the significance of building a consistent meditation practice and sets the stage for the comprehensive guide that follows.

It acknowledges the common challenges individuals face in establishing a regular meditation routine and emphasizes the transformative potential of a consistent practice. By understanding the importance of consistency, individuals can embark on their meditation journey with a clear sense of purpose and commitment.

Setting the Foundation for Your Practice

Understanding Your Motivation

Before embarking on a meditation journey, it's essential to understand your motivation. This section delves into the importance of clarifying why you want to meditate and what you hope to achieve through your practice.

We explore various motivations for meditation, from stress reduction and enhanced focus to personal growth and spiritual exploration. The guidance encourages individuals to identify their unique reasons for meditating and to keep these motivations in mind as they build their practice. By aligning their practice with their goals and intentions, individuals can maintain a sense of purpose and commitment.

Creating a Sacred Space

Having a dedicated space for meditation can greatly enhance your practice. This section delves into the concept of creating a sacred space and provides insights into its significance.

We discuss the elements of an ideal meditation space, including comfort, minimal distractions, and personal touches that evoke a sense of tranquility. The guidance offers practical tips on how to set up a meditation space in your home or office. By establishing a sacred space, individuals create an environment that supports their practice and serves as a reminder of their commitment to meditation.

Choosing Your Meditation Style

Exploring Different Meditation Styles

Meditation is a diverse practice with various styles and techniques. This section explores the wide array of meditation styles available, from mindfulness and loving-kindness meditation to transcendental meditation and Zen meditation.

We discuss the fundamental principles and practices associated with each style, highlighting their unique qualities and benefits. The guidance encourages individuals to explore different meditation styles and discover which resonates most with them. By experimenting with different styles, individuals can find a meditation approach that aligns with their preferences and needs.

Tailoring Your Practice

Once you've explored different meditation styles, it's important to tailor your practice to suit your preferences and goals. This section delves into the concept of tailoring your meditation practice and provides practical guidance on doing so.

We discuss how to adapt meditation techniques to fit your schedule, lifestyle, and comfort level. The guidance offers insights into modifying the duration of your meditation sessions, selecting appropriate postures, and incorporating variations that align with your personal preferences. By customizing your practice, you can make meditation a more accessible and enjoyable part of your life.

Building Consistency in Meditation

Establishing a Routine

Consistency in meditation is best achieved through the establishment of a routine. This section explores the importance of setting a regular schedule for your practice and offers practical strategies for doing so.

We discuss the benefits of routine, including how it helps create a habit of meditation and ensures that it becomes an integral part of your daily life. The guidance provides insights into setting a specific time for your practice, whether it's in the morning, during lunch breaks, or in the evening. By establishing a routine, individuals create a structure that supports their commitment to meditation.

Overcoming Resistance and Distractions

Resistance and distractions are common challenges in maintaining a consistent meditation practice. This section delves into the nature of resistance and distractions and offers practical strategies for overcoming them.

We explore how resistance can manifest as a reluctance to meditate or as an inner battle during meditation. The guidance provides insights into acknowledging resistance without judgment and developing self-compassion as a means to overcome it. We also discuss the role of distractions and offer techniques for working with them, including using anchors like the breath and mindful observation. By understanding these challenges and embracing effective strategies, individuals can navigate the path of consistency more skilfully.

Tracking Your Progress

Tracking your progress in meditation can be a powerful motivator for building consistency. This section delves into the concept of tracking your meditation practice and provides guidance on how to do so effectively.

We discuss various methods for tracking your practice, from meditation journals and apps to simple calendar notations. The guidance emphasizes the importance of setting achievable goals and celebrating milestones along the way. By tracking your progress, individuals can maintain a sense of accomplishment and motivation in their meditation journey.

Nurturing Your Practice

Seeking Guidance and Community

Meditation is a personal practice, but seeking guidance and community support can be valuable. This section explores the benefits of learning from experienced meditation teachers and connecting with like-minded individuals.

We discuss the role of meditation classes, workshops, and online resources in deepening your practice. The guidance offers insights into the potential benefits of meditation communities and how they can provide motivation and shared experiences. By seeking guidance and community support, individuals can enrich their meditation journey and maintain their commitment to consistency.

Cultivating Patience and Perseverance

Patience and perseverance are essential qualities in building a consistent meditation practice. This section delves into the role of these qualities in nurturing your practice.

We discuss the necessity of patience when encountering challenges and distractions in meditation. The guidance encourages individuals to cultivate perseverance, acknowledging that building a consistent practice is a journey with ups and downs. By embracing these qualities, individuals can navigate the inevitable ebbs and flows of their meditation journey with resilience and determination.

The Ongoing Journey of Meditation

As we conclude this comprehensive guide on building a consistent meditation practice, it's essential to reiterate that meditation is an ongoing journey. It is not about achieving perfection but about cultivating mindfulness and inner awareness.

The conclusion underscores the transformative potential of meditation, emphasizing the benefits of consistency, including reduced stress, enhanced focus, and greater overall well-being. It encourages individuals to approach meditation as a lifelong practice, one that evolves and deepens over time.

Ultimately, by setting a strong foundation, customizing your practice, and embracing practical strategies, you can build and maintain a consistent meditation practice that brings lasting peace and self-discovery.

Finding Time for Meditation in a Busy Schedule

In the whirlwind of modern life, with its endless to-do lists and packed schedules, finding time for meditation can seem like an insurmountable challenge. However, it's precisely in these busy moments that meditation can offer the greatest benefits. This exploration will delve into the practical strategies and mindset shifts that can help you carve out time for meditation, no matter how hectic your schedule may be.

The Busy Life Dilemma

In today's fast-paced world, we're constantly juggling multiple responsibilities, from work and family to social commitments and personal pursuits. The notion of adding another activity to our already crowded schedules can feel overwhelming. Yet, meditation is precisely what can provide solace and balance in the midst of life's hustle and bustle.

The introduction sets the stage for understanding the challenges of finding time for meditation in a busy schedule. It highlights the importance of shifting our mindset from viewing meditation as a task to viewing it as a necessity for our mental and emotional well-being.

The Benefits of Meditation for a Busy Life

One of the most significant advantages of meditation is stress reduction. In this section, we explore how meditation can help manage the daily stressors that come with a busy schedule. It highlights the scientific evidence supporting meditation's ability to reduce stress and enhance mental clarity, making it a valuable tool for busy individuals.

Stress Reduction and Mental Clarity

In the bustling, demanding world of today, it's not uncommon for stress to become a constant companion. The cumulative weight of responsibilities, deadlines, and obligations can take a toll on our mental and emotional well-being. This is where meditation shines as a solution. Scientific research has shown that regular meditation practice is associated with a significant reduction in stress levels.

Meditation is a journey inward, offering individuals a respite from the chaos of daily life. By quieting the mind, it provides a space for reflection and relaxation. As we delve deeper into this section, we explore the mechanisms behind how meditation reduces stress. We discuss the activation of the parasympathetic nervous system during meditation, which counters the "fight or flight" response triggered by stress. This shift in physiological state leads to a decrease in cortisol levels, the hormone associated with stress, and subsequently promotes a sense of calm and mental clarity.

Enhanced Focus and Productivity

In the modern world, distractions abound. The constant pinging of notifications, the allure of social media, and the never-ending stream of information can lead to a scattered mind and reduced productivity. The capacity to focus on tasks has become a prized skill in our time. Here, meditation comes into play as a tool for improving focus and productivity.

This section delves into the scientific underpinnings of how meditation enhances cognitive function. It highlights the benefits of improved attention span, memory, and the ability to switch between tasks effectively. Meditation's impact on the brain, particularly the prefrontal cortex associated with executive functions, offers a pathway to increased productivity.

Research has shown that individuals who incorporate meditation into their routines often exhibit heightened cognitive abilities. They're better equipped to manage the demands of a busy schedule, maintain their concentration on tasks, and achieve a state of flow in their work. By developing greater cognitive control through meditation, individuals are better equipped to tackle their to-do lists efficiently.

Strategies for Finding Time for Meditation

Finding time for meditation amidst a packed schedule requires mindful time management. It's about setting priorities and making conscious choices about how you allocate your time. This section provides a detailed exploration of the principles of mindful time management.

We delve into the importance of defining your priorities and creating a clear hierarchy of tasks. By determining what truly matters to you, you can make choices that align with your values and well-being. We discuss the creation of to-do lists that offer structure and organization while also minimizing the feeling of being overwhelmed. The guidance includes strategies for eliminating time-wasting activities, recognizing the value of setting boundaries, and learning the art of saying "no" to non-essential commitments. These strategies form the foundation for finding time for meditation within a busy schedule.

Micro-Meditations

Micro-meditations, brief and focused meditation practices, represent an ingenious solution for busy individuals. They provide an accessible way to integrate meditation into a hectic routine. In this section, we delve into the world of micro-meditations, exploring their potential and practicality.

We discuss the versatility of micro-meditations, emphasizing that they can be practiced in short breaks, during waiting times, or as transitions between tasks. These brief moments of meditation don't require an elaborate setup or a quiet space. Instead, they are designed to be seamlessly incorporated into the flow of daily life.

The guidance encourages individuals to embrace the power of micro-meditations in creating moments of mindfulness amidst the hustle and bustle. Whether it's a one-minute mindful breathing exercise or a moment of gratitude, micro-meditations can serve as a lifeline to greater presence and well-being.

Morning and Evening Rituals

Morning and evening rituals are another strategy for finding time for meditation. These rituals offer structure and consistency in your daily routine, creating designated slots for meditation. In this section, we explore the concept of morning and evening meditation rituals and their benefits.

We discuss the idea of using meditation to frame the day, setting intentions in the morning, and finding calm and closure in the evening. The guidance provides insights into creating a conducive environment for meditation within these rituals. Morning rituals can include meditation to start the day with mindfulness and clarity, while evening rituals may involve practices to unwind and reflect on the day's experiences.

The section emphasizes that these rituals need not be time-consuming but should be anchored in mindfulness. They serve as bookends to your day, reminding you of the importance of finding time for meditation and fostering a sense of balance in your life.

Making Meditation a Non-Negotiable

A fundamental mindset shift required for finding time for meditation is to view meditation as a non-negotiable aspect of self-care. In a busy life, it's easy to prioritize external demands and commitments over one's well-being. This section underscores the significance of reversing this trend and placing self-care, including meditation, at the forefront of your priorities.

We explore the concept of self-compassion and the importance of acknowledging your need for moments of reflection and tranquility. It's about recognizing that meditation is not a luxury but a necessity for your overall well-being. The guidance encourages individuals to shift their perspective and commit to making meditation an integral part of their daily routines.

Letting Go of Perfectionism

In the pursuit of finding time for meditation, it's essential to let go of perfectionism. The idea that meditation must be a flawless, uninterrupted experience can become a barrier. This section delves into the concept of embracing imperfection in meditation.

Meditation is not about achieving a flawless state of mind but about embracing the process and the journey. We discuss the importance of acknowledging that every meditation session may not be serene, and that's perfectly fine. By letting go of perfectionism, individuals can release the pressure to be an expert meditator and allow themselves to be beginners in the practice.

The guidance encourages individuals to be gentle with themselves and recognize that the simple act of showing up for meditation, regardless of the outcome, is a significant step towards finding time for meditation in a busy life.

Nurturing Your Inner Sanctuary

As we conclude this exploration, it's essential to reiterate the transformative potential of finding time for meditation in a busy schedule. The benefits of reduced stress, enhanced focus, and increased productivity are profound.

In the midst of a hectic life, meditation serves as an inner sanctuary, offering moments of tranquility and self-reflection. By incorporating the strategies and mindset shifts discussed in this exploration, individuals can make meditation an essential part of their daily routines.

Ultimately, finding time for meditation in a busy schedule is not about adding another item to your to-do list; it's about nurturing your inner well-being and achieving a sense of balance and presence in a busy world.

Beyond Meditation: Holistic Wellness

Meditation is a powerful tool for cultivating mental and emotional well-being, but holistic wellness encompasses a broader spectrum of practices and lifestyle choices that contribute to overall health. In this comprehensive guide, we explore the concept of holistic wellness, covering a range of aspects that go beyond meditation. From nutrition and exercise to mindfulness in daily life, this guide provides insights and practical strategies for achieving a state of balance, vitality, and optimal well-being.

The Holistic Approach to Wellness

Holistic wellness is a comprehensive perspective that recognizes the interconnectedness of physical, mental, emotional, and spiritual well-being. While meditation plays a vital role in nurturing mental and emotional health, it is just one piece of the puzzle in achieving holistic wellness. The introduction sets the stage for the guide, emphasizing the importance of looking at wellness from a holistic perspective and exploring various facets that contribute to a well-rounded and balanced life.

It acknowledges that a holistic approach is not about perfection but about making informed and sustainable choices that contribute to overall well-being. By embracing the principles of holistic wellness, individuals can create a roadmap for a fulfilling and vital life.

Nutrition for Wellness

Nutrition is a cornerstone of holistic wellness. This section delves into the role of nutrition in nourishing your body and mind. We discuss the importance of a balanced and diverse diet, rich in whole foods, and how it can impact physical health, mental clarity, and emotional balance.

The guidance offers insights into mindful eating and provides practical strategies for making healthier food choices. It emphasizes the significance of listening to your body's cues, eating intuitively, and maintaining a sustainable relationship with food. By understanding the connection between nutrition and holistic wellness, individuals can foster a sense of vitality and overall health.

Hydration and Wellness

Proper hydration is often overlooked, yet it is a crucial aspect of well-being. This section explores the impact of hydration on physical and mental health. We discuss the importance of water in maintaining bodily functions, including cognitive performance and emotional stability.

The guidance provides practical tips on staying hydrated and emphasizes the need to develop a consistent and balanced approach to water intake. By recognizing the role of hydration in holistic wellness, individuals can enhance their physical and mental vitality.

Exercise for Well-Being

Regular exercise is a fundamental component of holistic wellness. This section delves into the role of physical activity in promoting mental and emotional health. We discuss the benefits of exercise, from reducing stress and anxiety to improving mood and cognitive function.

The guidance offers insights into finding an exercise routine that suits your lifestyle and preferences. It emphasizes the importance of consistent physical activity and encourages individuals to view exercise as a form of self-care. By incorporating regular exercise, individuals can enhance their physical health and mental well-being.

Rest and Sleep

Quality rest and sleep are vital for overall wellness. This section explores the impact of rest and sleep on mental and emotional health. We discuss the importance of restorative sleep in maintaining cognitive function and emotional balance.

The guidance provides practical strategies for improving sleep hygiene and enhancing the quality of rest. It emphasizes the role of relaxation techniques, mindfulness practices, and establishing a consistent sleep schedule. By recognizing the connection between rest and holistic wellness, individuals can optimize their mental and emotional vitality.

Integrating Mindfulness into Everyday Activities

Mindfulness is not limited to formal meditation sessions; it can be integrated into daily life. This section explores the concept of mindfulness in everyday activities and its impact on mental and emotional well-being.

We discuss the practice of mindful awareness in daily routines, from eating and walking to communication and work. The guidance provides insights into the benefits of mindfulness in daily life, including improved focus, reduced stress, and enhanced emotional regulation. By embracing mindfulness as a way of life, individuals can infuse their daily activities with presence and balance.

Stress Management

Stress is a pervasive challenge in modern life, and effective stress management is a crucial aspect of holistic wellness. This section delves into the impact of stress on mental and emotional health and offers practical strategies for managing stress.

We discuss stress-reduction techniques, including deep breathing, progressive muscle relaxation, and time management. The guidance provides insights into the importance of self-care and setting boundaries to mitigate the effects of stress. By developing effective stress management practices, individuals can maintain mental and emotional equilibrium.

Social and Emotional Well-Being

Human connection and emotional support are essential for holistic wellness. This section explores the impact of social relationships on mental and emotional health.

We discuss the significance of nurturing positive relationships, cultivating a sense of belonging, and seeking emotional support when needed. The guidance provides insights into the importance of open communication, empathy, and setting boundaries in relationships. By recognizing the role of social and emotional well-being, individuals can enhance their overall mental and emotional vitality.

The Role of Nutrition in Stress Management

Stress is an inevitable part of modern life, and it can take a toll on both your mental and physical well-being. While meditation, mindfulness, and other stress-reduction techniques play a significant role in managing stress, it's important not to overlook the critical connection between nutrition and stress management. What you eat has a profound impact on your ability to cope with stress, and this comprehensive guide delves into the role of nutrition in stress management, providing insights and practical strategies for making informed dietary choices to promote resilience and emotional balance.

The Mind-Body Connection in Stress

Stress is not solely a mental or emotional phenomenon; it affects your entire body. The introduction highlights the interconnectedness of the mind and body in the context of stress and emphasizes that the foods you consume can either exacerbate or alleviate the impact of stress. It sets the stage for exploring the multifaceted role of nutrition in stress management and the transformative potential of making conscious dietary choices.

Nutrients that Impact Stress

The Stress-Reducing Power of Whole Foods

Whole foods, in their natural and unprocessed state, are a cornerstone of stress management. This section delves into the role of whole foods in reducing stress and promoting overall well-being. We discuss the nutrients found in whole foods, including vitamins, minerals, antioxidants, and fibre, that support physical and mental resilience.

The guidance offers practical tips on incorporating whole foods into your diet, such as choosing a variety of fruits and vegetables, opting for whole grains, and including lean proteins. By embracing whole foods, individuals can provide their bodies and minds with the essential nutrients needed to combat the effects of stress.

The Influence of Macronutrients on Stress

Macronutrients, including carbohydrates, fats, and proteins, have a significant influence on stress levels. This section explores the role of macronutrients in stress management and how they impact your energy levels, mood, and ability to cope with stress.

We discuss the importance of maintaining a balanced macronutrient intake and the benefits of complex carbohydrates in stabilizing blood sugar levels and regulating mood. The guidance provides insights into the healthy fats that support brain health and emotional well-being, as well as the role of protein in maintaining energy and mental focus. By understanding the influence of macronutrients, individuals can make dietary choices that enhance their ability to manage stress.

Nutrient-Rich Foods for Stress Management

Antioxidant-Rich Foods and Stress Reduction

Antioxidants are your body's natural defence against the harmful effects of stress. This section delves into the role of antioxidant-rich foods in reducing stress and promoting overall well-being. We discuss the connection between stress and oxidative stress, which can damage cells and lead to physical and mental health issues.

The guidance offers practical tips on incorporating antioxidant-rich foods into your diet, including colourful fruits and vegetables, nuts, and seeds. It emphasizes the importance of a diverse and balanced diet to ensure an adequate intake of antioxidants. By embracing antioxidant-rich foods, individuals can fortify their bodies against the detrimental effects of stress.

The Benefits of Omega-3 Fatty Acids

Omega-3 fatty acids, found in fatty fish, flaxseeds, and walnuts, are known for their powerful anti-inflammatory properties. This section explores the role of omega-3 fatty acids in stress management and their impact on brain health and emotional stability.

We discuss the influence of omega-3s on neurotransmitters and brain function, highlighting their potential to reduce stress and anxiety. The guidance offers practical tips on incorporating omega-3-rich foods into your diet and, if necessary, considering supplements. By embracing omega-3 fatty acids, individuals can enhance their brain health and emotional resilience in the face of stress.

The Connection Between Blood Sugar and Stress

Blood sugar levels play a crucial role in stress management. Fluctuations in blood sugar can lead to mood swings, irritability, and increased stress. This section delves into the connection between blood sugar regulation and stress and offers practical strategies for maintaining stable blood sugar levels.

We discuss the impact of refined carbohydrates and sugar on blood sugar spikes and crashes. The guidance provides insights into the benefits of complex carbohydrates, fibre, and mindful eating in stabilizing blood sugar levels and regulating mood. By understanding the relationship between blood sugar and stress, individuals can make dietary choices that support emotional balance.

The Role of Hydration in Stress Management

Proper hydration is often overlooked, yet it is a crucial aspect of maintaining physical and mental well-being in times of stress. This section explores the connection between hydration and stress management and how even mild dehydration can lead to increased stress and reduced cognitive function.

The guidance offers practical tips on staying hydrated and emphasizes the importance of listening to your body's cues. It discusses the role of water in maintaining cognitive performance, emotional stability, and overall well-being. By recognizing the influence of hydration on stress, individuals can enhance their ability to cope with life's challenges.

Mindful Eating and Emotional Well-Being

Mindful eating is a transformative practice that encourages individuals to develop a conscious and balanced relationship with food. This section explores the concept of mindful eating and its impact on emotional well-being and stress management.

We discuss the practice of mindful awareness in eating, which includes savouring each bite, listening to your body's hunger and fullness cues, and eating without distractions. The guidance provides practical strategies for incorporating mindful eating into your daily life and emphasizes its role in reducing stress and promoting emotional balance. By embracing mindful eating, individuals can develop a healthier and more positive relationship with food, one that supports their ability to cope with stress.

Emotional Eating and Stress Reduction

Emotional eating, or eating in response to emotional stress, is a common behaviour that can have a detrimental impact on well-being. This section delves into the concept of emotional eating, its triggers, and its connection to stress.

We discuss the importance of recognizing emotional eating patterns and the role of self-awareness in managing this behaviour. The guidance offers insights into alternative coping strategies for stress, such as practicing mindfulness, seeking social support, and engaging in stress-reduction techniques. By understanding the connection between emotions and eating, individuals can make conscious choices to reduce emotional eating and support their emotional well-being.

Making Informed Dietary Choices for Stress Management

As we conclude this comprehensive guide on the role of nutrition in stress management, it's essential to reiterate the transformative potential of making informed dietary choices. Nutrition is a powerful tool that can either exacerbate or alleviate the impact of stress.

The conclusion underscores the interconnectedness of physical and mental well-being in the context of stress and the importance of embracing a holistic approach to wellness. By incorporating the principles discussed in this guide, individuals can make dietary choices that foster resilience, emotional balance, and a greater capacity to manage stress effectively.

Ultimately, the role of nutrition in stress management extends beyond mere sustenance; it becomes a conscious and empowering choice that contributes to a more balanced and fulfilling life.

Seeking Professional Support

In some cases, seeking professional support is a vital aspect of holistic wellness. This section delves into the importance of reaching out to healthcare professionals and mental health experts when needed.

We discuss the role of therapy, counselling, and medical treatment in maintaining mental and emotional health. The guidance emphasizes the importance of recognizing when professional support is necessary and reducing the stigma surrounding mental health care. By seeking professional support, individuals can address mental and emotional challenges and achieve a state of holistic well-being.

Embracing Holistic Wellness

As we conclude this comprehensive guide on holistic wellness, it's essential to reiterate the transformative potential of embracing a holistic approach to well-being. Holistic wellness is about recognizing the interconnectedness of physical, mental, emotional, and spiritual health.

The conclusion underscores the importance of making informed and sustainable choices that contribute to overall well-being. By incorporating the principles of holistic wellness, individuals can create a balanced and fulfilling life that nurtures their mental and emotional health while promoting vitality and self-discovery.

Ultimately, beyond meditation, holistic wellness offers a path to a more fulfilling and vibrant life, where well-being is not limited to one aspect but encompasses the entire spectrum of human experience.

Exercise for Stress Reduction: A Comprehensive Guide

Exercise is a powerful and natural way to reduce stress, promote overall well-being, and improve mental health. In this comprehensive guide, we'll explore the numerous benefits of exercise for stress reduction, providing insights and practical strategies for incorporating physical activity into your daily life to manage and alleviate stress effectively.

Introduction: The Connection Between Exercise and Stress

The introduction sets the stage by highlighting the inextricable link between exercise and stress reduction. It emphasizes that exercise is not just about physical fitness but also plays a crucial role in mental and emotional health. By understanding this connection, individuals can embark on their journey to use exercise as a tool for stress reduction.

Understanding the Stress-Reducing Mechanisms of Exercise

Exercise triggers the release of endorphins, which are natural chemicals in the brain that act as mood elevators and pain relievers. This section delves into the science of how exercise stimulates the release of endorphins and other neurotransmitters, such as dopamine and serotonin, which play a significant role in stress reduction.

The guidance offers insights into how these chemicals improve mood, alleviate stress, and provide a sense of well-being. By understanding the neurobiological mechanisms at play, individuals can appreciate how exercise positively impacts their mental state.

The Impact on the HPA Axis

The hypothalamic-pituitary-adrenal (HPA) axis is a key player in the body's stress response. Regular exercise can help regulate this axis, reducing the production of stress hormones like cortisol. This section explores the interaction between exercise and the HPA axis, emphasizing the role of physical activity in managing stress.

We discuss how exercise can disrupt the cycle of chronic stress and the potential benefits for individuals dealing with stress-related conditions. The guidance provides practical insights into how to harness exercise to modulate the HPA axis effectively.

The Benefits of Exercise for Stress Reduction

Reduced Perceived Stress

One of the most immediate benefits of exercise is a reduction in perceived stress. This section delves into how physical activity can help individuals feel less stressed and anxious.

We discuss the impact of exercise on the autonomic nervous system, which controls the body's stress response, and how regular activity can help balance it. The guidance offers practical tips on integrating exercise into one's daily routine to experience a tangible reduction in perceived stress.

Enhanced Mood and Emotional Well-Being

Exercise has a profound impact on mood and emotional well-being. This section explores how physical activity can help alleviate symptoms of anxiety and depression, and improve overall emotional health.

We discuss the role of endorphins and other mood-enhancing chemicals in reducing symptoms of mood disorders. The guidance offers insights into the importance of consistency in exercise routines to maintain emotional balance. By understanding how exercise enhances mood and emotional well-being, individuals can harness this natural remedy for stress reduction.

Types of Exercise for Stress Reduction

Aerobic exercise, such as running, swimming, and cycling, is known for its stress-reducing benefits. This section delves into the advantages of aerobic exercise in managing stress and improving overall mental health.

We discuss the role of aerobic exercise in reducing anxiety, depression, and stress symptoms. The guidance provides practical strategies for incorporating aerobic exercise into one's life, including setting realistic goals and creating a sustainable routine.

Mind-Body Practices

Mind-body practices, like yoga, Tai Chi, and Pilates, combine physical movement with mindfulness and relaxation techniques. This section explores the unique benefits of mind-body practices in stress reduction.

We discuss how mind-body practices can help individuals connect with their bodies and minds, reducing stress and promoting emotional balance. The guidance offers insights into choosing the right mind-body practice and integrating it into daily life for maximum stress reduction.

Making Exercise a Consistent Habit

Consistency is key when using exercise as a tool for stress reduction. This section delves into the importance of establishing a regular exercise routine.

We discuss the benefits of routine, including how it helps individuals become more attuned to their bodies and reduce stress over time. The guidance provides practical strategies for setting specific exercise goals and creating a dedicated space for physical activity. By establishing a routine, individuals can make exercise an integral part of their lives and diminish the impact of stress.

Overcoming Barriers and Staying Motivated

Exercise, like any habit, can come with its own set of challenges. This section explores common barriers to maintaining an exercise routine and provides practical strategies for overcoming them.

We discuss time constraints, motivation, and mental barriers that can deter individuals from regular exercise. The guidance offers insights into setting achievable goals, seeking social support, and staying motivated. By understanding the challenges of maintaining an exercise routine and embracing effective strategies, individuals can stay committed to using exercise as a tool for stress reduction.

Harnessing the Power of Exercise for Stress Reduction

As we conclude this comprehensive guide on exercise for stress reduction, it's essential to reiterate the transformative potential of physical activity. Exercise is not merely a means to improve physical fitness; it is a powerful tool for managing stress and promoting mental and emotional well-being.

The conclusion underscores the importance of making exercise a consistent part of one's routine and lifestyle. By incorporating the principles and strategies discussed in this guide, individuals can harness the natural stress-reducing benefits of exercise and improve their overall quality of life.

Sleep and Stress: The Crucial Connection

Sleep is a fundamental aspect of human well-being, and its quality and quantity are closely linked to our ability to manage stress. This comprehensive guide delves into the intricate relationship between sleep and stress, exploring how poor sleep can lead to heightened stress levels, and how effectively managing stress can, in turn, improve sleep quality. We'll provide insights and practical strategies for achieving better sleep and reducing stress to create a positive feedback loop for your overall well-being.

The Interplay Between Sleep and Stress

The introduction sets the stage for understanding the crucial connection between sleep and stress. It highlights that sleep and stress are intricately linked and that disruptions in one can adversely affect the other. This introduction emphasizes the importance of exploring the bi-directional relationship between sleep and stress and its profound impact on overall well-being.

How Stress Affects Sleep

Stress-Related Sleep Disturbances

Stress can lead to a range of sleep disturbances, such as difficulty falling asleep, staying asleep, or experiencing restorative sleep. This section delves into the various ways that stress negatively impacts sleep.

We discuss the role of stress hormones, such as cortisol, in disrupting sleep patterns and contributing to sleep disorders. The guidance offers practical insights into identifying stress-related sleep disturbances and their impact on overall health.

The Mind-Body Connection

Stress often originates in the mind but manifests in physical ways that can interfere with sleep. This section explores the mind-body connection and how it plays a significant role in sleep disturbances caused by stress.

We discuss the role of racing thoughts, muscle tension, and the physiological stress response in sleep disruption. The guidance provides practical strategies for managing these physical manifestations of stress to improve sleep quality.

The Impact of Sleep Deprivation on Stress

Poor sleep quality and sleep deprivation can exacerbate stress and make it more challenging to cope with life's demands. This section delves into how a lack of sleep can affect stress levels.

We discuss the impact of sleep deprivation on mood, cognitive function, and emotional regulation. The guidance offers insights into the importance of sleep for stress resilience and provides practical strategies for getting better sleep.

Sleep as Emotional Processing

During deep sleep, the brain processes and consolidates emotional experiences. This section explores the role of sleep in emotional processing and its connection to stress.

We discuss how adequate sleep allows the brain to work through emotional challenges, reducing the emotional burden and stress response. The guidance offers practical tips for improving the emotional processing aspects of sleep, which can positively impact stress management.

Practical Strategies for Better Sleep and Stress Management

Sleep Hygiene

Sleep hygiene refers to practices and habits that promote better sleep. This section delves into the concept of sleep hygiene and its importance in improving sleep quality and managing stress.

We discuss the role of a consistent sleep schedule, a comfortable sleep environment, and the impact of technology on sleep. The guidance offers practical tips for implementing a sleep hygiene routine that contributes to better sleep and reduced stress.

Stress Reduction Techniques

Effective stress management is key to achieving better sleep. This section explores various stress reduction techniques that can help individuals cope with stress and improve sleep quality.

We discuss mindfulness, meditation, progressive muscle relaxation, and deep breathing exercises. The guidance offers insights into how these techniques can calm the mind and reduce stress, promoting better sleep.

Breaking the Cycle of Sleep and Stress

Breaking the cycle of poor sleep and heightened stress is essential for overall well-being. This section delves into the power of creating a positive feedback loop between sleep and stress management.

We discuss how improving sleep quality can reduce stress, and how effectively managing stress can lead to better sleep. The guidance offers practical strategies for creating a positive feedback loop, which can significantly enhance both sleep and stress management.

Embracing the Symbiotic Relationship

As we conclude this comprehensive guide on the crucial connection between sleep and stress, it's essential to recognize the symbiotic relationship between the two. Sleep and stress are intertwined, and their management is pivotal for overall well-being.

The conclusion underscores the transformative potential of making informed choices to improve sleep and manage stress. By incorporating the insights and strategies presented in this guide, individuals can create a harmonious relationship between sleep and stress, ultimately leading to a more balanced and healthy life.

Seeking Support: Social and Emotional Well-Being

Social and emotional well-being is a crucial aspect of overall mental health. In this comprehensive guide, we explore the significance of seeking support from social and emotional networks, addressing the importance of positive relationships and emotional well-being for individuals' mental health. We provide insights and practical strategies for nurturing these connections to foster resilience and maintain a sense of belonging and emotional balance.

The Role of Support in Well-Being

The introduction emphasizes the vital role of support in social and emotional well-being. It highlights the interconnectedness of mental health with social and emotional networks, underlining that seeking support is not a sign of weakness but a valuable resource for personal growth and well-being.

Building and Nurturing Positive Relationships

Positive relationships are a cornerstone of social and emotional well-being. This section delves into the significance of cultivating and maintaining healthy relationships in our lives.

We discuss the impact of positive relationships on mental health, including reduced stress and increased emotional stability. The guidance provides insights into the qualities of healthy relationships, such as trust, respect, and open communication. It also offers practical tips for building and nurturing these connections to enhance social and emotional well-being.

The Role of Empathy and Communication

Effective communication and empathy are essential in fostering positive relationships. This section explores how the skills of empathy and effective communication contribute to emotional well-being and support.

We discuss the importance of active listening, nonverbal cues, and empathy in understanding and connecting with others. The guidance offers insights into how these skills can improve relationships and enhance emotional well-being. It also provides practical strategies for honing these abilities in our interactions with others.

Recognizing the Need for Emotional Support

Acknowledging when emotional support is needed is a crucial step in maintaining well-being. This section delves into the importance of recognizing the need for emotional support and seeking help when required.

We discuss the common signs of needing emotional support, such as increased stress, anxiety, or feelings of isolation. The guidance provides insights into the benefits of reaching out to trusted individuals or professionals, such as therapists or counsellors, when dealing with emotional challenges. It also offers practical tips for overcoming any reluctance or stigma surrounding seeking emotional support.

The Role of Therapists and Counsellors

Therapists and counsellors play a valuable role in providing emotional support and facilitating mental health. This section explores the significance of seeking professional help and the role of therapists and counsellors in supporting emotional well-being.

We discuss the types of therapy, such as cognitive-behavioural therapy and talk therapy, and their potential benefits. The guidance offers insights into how therapy can help individuals navigate emotional challenges, develop coping strategies, and enhance emotional well-being. It also provides practical information on finding the right therapist or counsellor.

The Importance of Social Connections

Social connections, such as friendships and community involvement, are essential for emotional well-being. This section delves into the significance of nurturing social connections for mental health.

We discuss the impact of social engagement on reducing stress, enhancing emotional stability, and providing a sense of belonging. The guidance provides insights into the qualities of healthy social connections and offers practical strategies for building and maintaining a supportive social network.

The Role of Community Involvement

Engaging in community and social activities can have a positive impact on well-being. This section explores the role of community involvement in nurturing social connections and promoting emotional stability.

We discuss the potential benefits of participating in community events, volunteering, and building a sense of belonging. The guidance offers practical insights into how community involvement can foster social connections and enhance emotional well-being. It also provides tips for individuals to find activities that align with their interests and values.

Embracing Support for Holistic Well-Being

As we conclude this comprehensive guide on seeking support for social and emotional well-being, it's essential to recognize the transformative potential of embracing support from our social and emotional networks. Support is a valuable resource for personal growth, resilience, and emotional balance.

The conclusion underscores the importance of making informed choices to nurture positive relationships, seek emotional support when needed, and engage in social connections. By incorporating the insights and strategies discussed in this guide, individuals can foster their social and emotional well-being, ultimately leading to a more balanced and healthy life.

Mindfulness in Action: Bringing Presence to Daily Life

Mindfulness is not just a practice confined to meditation sessions; it can be a way of life. In this comprehensive guide, we explore how to bring mindfulness into your daily activities, fostering a sense of presence and awareness. We provide insights and practical strategies for practicing mindfulness in action, allowing you to cultivate a deeper connection to the present moment and promote emotional balance and well-being.

The Essence of Mindfulness in Action

The introduction sets the stage for understanding the essence of mindfulness in action. It emphasizes that mindfulness is not limited to formal meditation but can be integrated into everyday activities. This introduction highlights the transformative potential of practicing mindfulness in action for mental and emotional well-being.

Cultivating Mindfulness in Everyday Activities

Eating is one of the most accessible daily activities in which to practice mindfulness. This section delves into the practice of mindful eating and its potential benefits for promoting awareness and emotional balance.

We discuss the importance of savouring each bite, paying attention to the Flavors and textures of food, and being present during meals. The guidance provides practical strategies for incorporating mindful eating into your daily life to enhance your connection with the present moment and support emotional well-being.

Mindful Walking and Movement

Movement can be a powerful vehicle for mindfulness. This section explores the practice of mindful walking and other forms of mindful movement, such as yoga and Tai Chi.

We discuss the role of breath and body awareness in movement practices and their potential to cultivate presence and emotional balance. The guidance offers practical tips for integrating mindful walking and movement into your daily routine to promote a deeper connection with your body and surroundings.

Mindful Listening and Speaking

Effective communication involves not only what we say but how we listen. This section delves into the practice of mindful listening and speaking, which can enhance our connections with others and promote emotional balance.

We discuss the importance of active listening, presence, and empathy in communication. The guidance provides practical insights into how mindfulness can improve the quality of conversations and relationships, leading to greater emotional well-being.

Mindful Digital Communication

In today's digital age, communication often takes place through screens. This section explores the practice of mindful digital communication and the importance of being present in our interactions in the online world.

We discuss the impact of constant connectivity on mental and emotional well-being and offer practical strategies for setting boundaries and being more mindful in your digital interactions. By embracing mindfulness in digital communication, individuals can foster a healthier relationship with technology and improve their emotional balance.

Mindful Work Habits

Work occupies a significant portion of our lives, making it an ideal space for practicing mindfulness. This section delves into the importance of cultivating mindful work habits and how they can enhance productivity, reduce stress, and improve emotional well-being.

We discuss the benefits of staying present in work tasks, taking short mindful breaks, and minimizing multitasking. The guidance offers practical strategies for incorporating mindfulness into your work routine, ultimately leading to greater work satisfaction and emotional balance.

Mindful Stress Management at Work

Stress is a common challenge in the workplace. This section explores the role of mindfulness in managing stress at work and maintaining emotional well-being.

We discuss stress reduction techniques, such as deep breathing and mindfulness meditation, and how they can be applied during the workday. The guidance offers practical insights into using mindfulness to cope with workplace stress and improve overall well-being.

Embracing Mindfulness in Action

As we conclude this comprehensive guide on mindfulness in action, it's essential to recognize the transformative potential of embracing mindfulness in your daily activities. Mindfulness is not confined to meditation but can be integrated into everyday life, fostering a deeper connection with the present moment and promoting emotional balance.

The conclusion underscores the importance of making informed choices to practice mindfulness in action, whether during meals, movement, communication, or work. By incorporating the insights and strategies discussed in this guide, individuals can lead a more mindful, balanced, and emotionally fulfilling life.

Mindful Communication: Navigating Relationships in the Digital Age

In today's digital era, effective and mindful communication is crucial for nurturing relationships and maintaining healthy connections with others. This comprehensive guide explores the challenges and opportunities of communication in the digital age, emphasizing the importance of mindfulness in fostering meaningful and fulfilling relationships. We provide insights and practical strategies for practicing mindful communication, allowing you to navigate the complexities of digital relationships with empathy, presence, and emotional balance.

The Digital Transformation of Communication

The introduction sets the stage by highlighting the significant changes in communication brought about by the digital age. It underscores the growing importance of mindful communication in the context of online interactions, emphasizing that the principles of mindfulness are essential for maintaining authentic and meaningful relationships in the digital realm.

The Art of Mindful Listening and Speaking

Mindful listening is a foundational aspect of communication. This section delves into the practice of mindful listening in the digital age and its potential to enhance online interactions.

We discuss the challenges of digital distractions and the importance of being fully present when engaging in online conversations. The guidance provides practical strategies for developing active listening skills in the digital realm, fostering deeper connections and more empathetic communication.

Mindful Speaking and Expressing Online

Effective and mindful expression is equally essential in digital communication. This section explores the practice of mindful speaking and how it can improve the quality of your online interactions.

We discuss the impact of tone, choice of words, and emotional intelligence in digital conversations. The guidance offers practical insights into using mindfulness to express yourself authentically and empathetically online, ultimately promoting healthier and more meaningful connections.

The Role of Empathy in Online Relationships

Empathy is a cornerstone of healthy relationships. This section delves into the role of empathy in digital relationships and the importance of understanding and sharing the emotions of others in the online world.

We discuss the challenges of perceiving and expressing empathy online and offer practical strategies for developing and practicing digital empathy. By embracing empathy in your digital interactions, you can build stronger and more compassionate online relationships.

Navigating Online Conflict with Empathy

Online conflicts are common, but they can be navigated mindfully with empathy. This section explores the role of empathy in resolving conflicts and misunderstandings in digital relationships.

We discuss the challenges of empathy during online disagreements and offer practical insights into de-escalating tension with a mindful and empathetic approach. By approaching conflicts in the digital realm with empathy, individuals can maintain healthier and more harmonious online relationships.

The Need for Digital Boundaries

In the digital age, setting boundaries is essential for maintaining well-being and healthy relationships. This section delves into the importance of defining digital boundaries and ensuring they align with your values and needs.

We discuss the challenges of boundary-setting in a hyper-connected world and offer practical strategies for establishing and communicating your digital boundaries. By setting clear digital boundaries, individuals can navigate online relationships more effectively and reduce the risk of burnout and emotional drain.

Communicating Boundaries Mindfully

Once boundaries are established, mindful communication is essential in maintaining them. This section explores the role of mindful communication in expressing and upholding digital boundaries.

We discuss the potential challenges of communicating boundaries with empathy and assertiveness, ensuring that they are respected. The guidance provides practical insights into using mindfulness to maintain healthy online relationships while respecting your personal limits.

Fostering Authentic Connections in the Digital Age

As we conclude this comprehensive guide on mindful communication in the digital age, it's essential to recognize the transformative potential of embracing mindfulness in your online relationships. Mindful communication is the key to fostering authentic, meaningful, and fulfilling connections in the digital realm.

The conclusion underscores the importance of making informed choices to practice mindful listening and speaking, empathetic communication, and setting and communicating digital boundaries. By incorporating the insights and strategies discussed in this guide, individuals can navigate digital relationships with empathy, presence, and emotional balance, ultimately leading to a more authentic and harmonious online life.

Mindful Parenting: Balancing Technology and Family

In an increasingly digital world, mindful parenting has become more important than ever. This comprehensive guide explores the challenges and opportunities of raising children in the digital age. It emphasizes the importance of mindfulness in parenting, providing insights and practical strategies for finding a balance between technology and family life. By practicing mindful parenting, you can foster healthy relationships, promote emotional well-being, and navigate the complexities of modern technology.

Parenting in the Digital Age

The introduction sets the stage by highlighting the profound changes in family life brought about by technology. It emphasizes that parenting in the digital age requires a new set of skills, including mindfulness, to guide children through this technological landscape. The introduction underscores the transformative potential of mindful parenting for building strong family connections and nurturing emotional well-being.

Understanding the Impact of Technology on Children

The digital age has introduced children to a world of screens and connectivity. This section delves into the impact of technology on children and their development, including both positive and negative effects.

We discuss the potential benefits of technology in education and entertainment, as well as the challenges, such as screen addiction and cyberbullying. The guidance provides insights into the importance of understanding the role of technology in children's lives to make informed parenting decisions.

The Impact of Parental Technology Use

Parents' technology use also plays a crucial role in family life. This section explores the impact of parental technology use on children and their relationships.

We discuss the potential consequences of distracted parenting and the importance of modeling healthy technology habits. The guidance offers practical strategies for mindful technology use as parents, ensuring that children feel valued and heard in the digital age.

Mindful Parenting Strategies

Cultivating Mindful Presence

Mindful presence is a cornerstone of mindful parenting. This section delves into the practice of being fully present with your children, irrespective of distractions or digital devices.

We discuss the challenges of maintaining mindful presence in a hyper-connected world and offer practical insights into techniques for tuning into your children's needs and emotions. By cultivating mindful presence, parents can build stronger connections and promote emotional well-being.

Setting Boundaries and Limits

Setting boundaries and limits around technology use is essential for balancing family life. This section explores the importance of defining technology guidelines for children and the family.

We discuss the challenges of setting and enforcing boundaries in the digital age and provide practical strategies for creating and communicating family technology rules. By setting clear boundaries, parents can maintain a healthy balance between screen time and real-life interactions.

Teaching Responsible Technology Use

Digital literacy is a vital skill in the modern world. This section delves into the importance of teaching children responsible technology use, including online safety and ethical behaviour.

We discuss the challenges of balancing freedom and safety in digital spaces and provide practical insights into teaching children to be responsible digital citizens. By fostering digital literacy, parents can equip their children with the skills needed to navigate the digital age mindfully and safely.

Encouraging Offline Activities

Offline activities are essential for promoting a healthy balance between technology and family life. This section explores the importance of encouraging children to engage in non-screen activities.

We discuss the potential challenges of competing with screens for children's attention and offer practical strategies for promoting offline hobbies and family bonding. By encouraging offline activities, parents can create a well-rounded and emotionally rich family environment.

Nurturing Mindful Family Connections

As we conclude this comprehensive guide on mindful parenting in the digital age, it's essential to recognize the transformative potential of practicing mindfulness in your family life. Mindful parenting is the key to balancing technology and family, fostering healthy relationships, promoting emotional well-being, and navigating the complexities of the modern digital landscape.

The conclusion underscores the importance of making informed choices to be fully present, set boundaries, and foster digital literacy in your children's lives. By incorporating the insights and strategies discussed in this guide, parents can nurture mindful family connections, ultimately leading to a more balanced, meaningful, and emotionally fulfilling family life.

Mindful Work: Reducing Stress in the Workplace

In the fast-paced and demanding world of the modern workplace, stress has become a common companion for many. This comprehensive guide explores how mindfulness can be integrated into the work environment to reduce stress, improve overall well-being, and enhance job satisfaction. We provide insights and practical strategies for practicing mindfulness at work, allowing you to create a more harmonious and stress-free professional life.

The Modern Workplace and Stress

The introduction sets the stage by highlighting the prevalence of stress in the modern workplace. It emphasizes the impact of stress on employees' well-being and job performance and introduces the concept of mindfulness as a tool for stress reduction and improved workplace satisfaction.

The Impact of Workplace Stress

The workplace is a significant source of stress for many individuals. This section delves into the various ways in which work-related stress affects employees' mental and physical health, job performance, and overall job satisfaction.

We discuss the symptoms of workplace stress, such as burnout, anxiety, and reduced productivity. The guidance offers insights into the importance of recognizing and understanding workplace stress to address it effectively.

The Role of Work Environment

The work environment plays a crucial role in shaping employees' stress levels. This section explores how factors such as job demands, job security, and company culture can impact workplace stress.

We discuss how work-related stress can be exacerbated by high workloads, unrealistic expectations, and a lack of work-life balance. The guidance provides practical strategies for assessing and improving the work environment to reduce stress.

Mindfulness as a Stress Reduction Tool

Mindfulness is increasingly recognized as a powerful tool for reducing workplace stress. This section delves into the benefits of mindfulness in managing stress and enhancing well-being at work.

We discuss the impact of mindfulness on stress reduction, emotional regulation, and job satisfaction. The guidance offers insights into the importance of integrating mindfulness practices into the workday to reap these benefits.

Improved Focus and Productivity

Mindfulness also enhances focus and productivity, contributing to overall job satisfaction. This section explores how practicing mindfulness at work can lead to improved concentration and efficiency.

We discuss the role of mindfulness in reducing distractions, multitasking, and improving task completion. The guidance provides practical strategies for incorporating mindfulness techniques into work routines to boost focus and productivity.

Practical Mindfulness Strategies at Work

Mindful Breathing and Mini-Meditations

Simple mindfulness exercises, such as mindful breathing and mini-meditations, can be practiced discreetly at work to reduce stress. This section delves into the importance of these techniques and their potential benefits.

We discuss the challenges of finding moments for mindfulness at work and offer practical insights into incorporating short, mindful breaks into the workday. By practicing mindful breathing and mini-meditations, employees can effectively reduce stress and maintain a sense of balance.

Mindful Communication and Conflict Resolution

Mindful communication is another valuable tool for reducing workplace stress. This section explores the role of mindfulness in enhancing communication and resolving conflicts in the professional environment.

We discuss how mindfulness can improve active listening, empathy, and effective communication with colleagues and superiors. The guidance provides practical insights into using mindfulness to foster positive relationships and navigate workplace conflicts with equanimity.

Embracing Mindfulness at Work

As we conclude this comprehensive guide on practicing mindfulness at work to reduce stress and enhance job satisfaction, it's essential to recognize the transformative potential of mindfulness in the workplace. Mindful work is not only about stress reduction but also about creating a more harmonious and satisfying professional life.

The conclusion underscores the importance of making informed choices to integrate mindfulness into your work routine. By incorporating the insights and strategies discussed in this guide, employees can experience reduced workplace stress, improved job satisfaction, and a more balanced and fulfilling professional life.

Mindfulness in Creativity and Problem Solving

Creativity and effective problem-solving are critical skills in the modern world. This comprehensive guide explores how mindfulness can be harnessed to enhance your creative thinking and problem-solving abilities. We delve into the interplay between mindfulness and creativity, offering practical strategies for incorporating mindfulness techniques into your creative endeavors and decision-making processes.

The Connection Between Mindfulness, Creativity, and Problem Solving

The introduction sets the stage by highlighting the significance of creativity and problem-solving in personal and professional life. It introduces the concept of mindfulness as a powerful tool for enhancing these skills and emphasizes the potential for transformative change through mindful creativity and problem-solving.

Understanding Creativity and Problem Solving

Exploring the Creative Process

Creativity is a multifaceted process that involves ideation, incubation, illumination, and verification. This section delves into the creative process and the stages involved in generating novel and valuable ideas.

We discuss the challenges that individuals face in different stages of the creative process, from generating ideas to implementing them. The guidance offers insights into understanding the complexities of creativity and the potential for mindfulness to enhance it.

The Art of Problem Solving

Problem solving is an integral part of life. This section explores the concept of problem solving, its various approaches, and the importance of effective decision-making in both personal and professional contexts.

We discuss the challenges that people encounter when faced with complex problems and decisions. The guidance provides practical strategies for improving problem-solving skills through mindfulness.

The Role of Mindfulness in Creativity and Problem Solving

Mindfulness can serve as a catalyst for creativity by promoting an open and non-judgmental mindset. This section delves into the role of mindfulness in stimulating creativity and enhancing the quality of creative ideas.

We discuss how mindfulness encourages a deeper connection with the present moment, reduces mental chatter, and fosters a heightened awareness of internal and external experiences. The guidance offers insights into the importance of mindfulness for enhancing creativity and provides practical strategies for incorporating mindfulness into the creative process.

Mindfulness for Effective Problem Solving

Mindfulness can also be a powerful tool for effective problem solving. This section explores the ways in which mindfulness can improve decision-making and problem-solving abilities.

We discuss how mindfulness can enhance cognitive flexibility, reduce stress, and improve focus, all of which are vital for effective problem solving. The guidance provides practical insights into applying mindfulness techniques to decision-making processes.

Practical Mindfulness Strategies for Creativity and Problem Solving

Mindful meditation is a valuable practice for enhancing creativity. This section delves into the practice of mindful meditation and its potential benefits for stimulating creative thinking.

We discuss various meditation techniques, such as focused attention and open monitoring meditation, and their impact on creative ideation. The guidance offers practical strategies for incorporating mindful meditation into your creative process.

Mindfulness for Effective Decision-Making

Mindfulness can improve decision-making and problem-solving by enhancing cognitive clarity and emotional regulation. This section explores the practical application of mindfulness techniques for effective decision-making.

We discuss the role of mindfulness in reducing cognitive biases, enhancing self-awareness, and promoting rational thinking. The guidance provides practical insights into using mindfulness for effective problem solving and decision-making.

Embracing Mindfulness for Creative Excellence

As we conclude this comprehensive guide on the role of mindfulness in creativity and problem solving, it's essential to recognize the transformative potential of embracing mindfulness in these domains. Mindfulness is not only about enhancing creative thinking and problem-solving but also about creating a more balanced and fulfilling personal and professional life.

The conclusion underscores the importance of making informed choices to incorporate mindfulness techniques into your creative endeavours and decision-making processes. By incorporating the insights and strategies discussed in this guide, individuals can experience a significant improvement in their creative thinking and problem-solving skills, ultimately leading to a more creative, balanced, and fulfilling life.

The Digital Age and Spirituality: Finding Meaning in a Connected World

The emergence of the digital age has brought profound changes to the way we live, work, and connect with the world. It has also raised significant questions about how these changes impact our spiritual lives and quest for meaning. This comprehensive guide explores the relationship between the digital age and spirituality, examining both the challenges and opportunities presented by technology. We provide insights and practical strategies for finding and nurturing spirituality in a digitally connected world.

The Intersection of Technology and Spirituality

The introduction sets the stage by acknowledging the profound impact of the digital age on our lives and the various ways technology has reshaped our existence. It highlights the fundamental question of how spirituality can coexist with technology and emphasizes the need for balance in our digital lives.

Digital Distractions and Disconnection

One of the most significant challenges in the digital age is the constant bombardment of information and the distractions it can create. This section delves into the issues of digital distractions and how they can disconnect us from our spiritual selves.

We discuss the challenges of staying present and focused in a hyper-connected world. The guidance provides insights into the impact of these distractions on our spiritual well-being and offers practical strategies for regaining focus and presence.

The Paradox of Virtual Connectivity

While the digital age connects us virtually, it can sometimes lead to feelings of isolation and disconnection from the real world. This section explores the paradox of virtual connectivity and its impact on our sense of community and belonging.

We discuss how online relationships can be both enriching and isolating and the challenges of finding authentic connection in the digital realm. The guidance offers practical strategies for building and nurturing meaningful virtual and real-world relationships.

Opportunities and Integration

Digital Tools for Mindfulness and Meditation

Technology can also be a valuable tool for enhancing our spiritual practice. This section delves into the opportunities presented by digital tools for mindfulness and meditation.

We discuss the benefits of apps, online communities, and guided meditations in supporting our spiritual journeys. The guidance provides practical insights into how to integrate these tools effectively into our daily spiritual practices.

Online Spiritual Communities and Learning

The digital age has created opportunities for individuals to connect with like-minded people and access spiritual teachings from around the world. This section explores the role of online spiritual communities and learning platforms in enriching our spiritual lives.

We discuss the benefits of engaging with virtual communities, participating in online courses, and accessing spiritual wisdom. The guidance offers practical strategies for making the most of these opportunities while maintaining a balanced and grounded spiritual life.

Balancing the Digital and the Spiritual

Balancing the digital and the spiritual requires the establishment of digital boundaries. This section delves into the importance of setting limits on digital consumption to nurture our spiritual well-being.

We discuss the challenges of digital addiction and its impact on our spiritual lives. The guidance provides practical strategies for creating digital boundaries that promote spiritual growth and connection.

Mindful Technology Use

Integrating mindfulness into our technology use is essential for maintaining a spiritual life in the digital age. This section explores the practice of mindful technology use and its potential to enhance our overall well-being.

We discuss how mindfulness can improve our relationship with technology, making us more conscious of our choices and their impact on our spiritual journey. The guidance provides practical insights into incorporating mindfulness into our digital lives.

Embracing Spirituality in a Connected World

As we conclude this comprehensive guide on the digital age and spirituality, it's essential to recognize the transformative potential of embracing spirituality in a connected world. The digital age and spirituality are not mutually exclusive; they can coexist and even enhance one another.

The conclusion underscores the importance of making informed choices to balance our digital and spiritual lives effectively. By incorporating the insights and strategies discussed in this guide, individuals can nurture their spiritual well-being in the digital age, ultimately leading to a more connected, meaningful, and balanced life.

Spirituality in a Secular World: Rediscovering Meaning and Purpose

In a world that has become increasingly secular and focused on materialism, the need for spirituality has not diminished; it has evolved. This comprehensive guide explores the role of spirituality in a secular world, emphasizing the importance of finding meaning and purpose in our lives. We delve into the challenges and opportunities of practicing spirituality in a secular context and provide insights and practical strategies for those seeking a deeper connection with themselves, others, and the world around them.

Navigating Spirituality in a Secular Landscape

The introduction sets the stage by acknowledging the prevailing secular nature of the world and the unique challenges it poses to spiritual seekers. It highlights the enduring human quest for meaning and purpose and introduces the concept of spirituality as a powerful means to address this quest.

Challenges and Disconnections

In a secular world, individuals often face a disconnect between their inner spiritual yearnings and the prevailing materialistic and rationalistic ideologies. This section delves into the challenges of feeling spiritually disconnected in a secular environment.

We discuss the impact of secularism on individuals' sense of meaning, belonging, and purpose. The guidance provides insights into recognizing and addressing this spiritual disconnect and offers practical strategies for reconnecting with one's spirituality.

The Pursuit of Materialism and Its Shortcomings

Materialism is a dominant force in the secular world, with a focus on material wealth and success. This section explores the limitations of the materialistic pursuit and its impact on our spiritual lives.

We discuss the challenges of defining success solely in material terms and the emptiness that often accompanies such pursuits. The guidance provides practical insights into reevaluating one's values and priorities to find a more meaningful and spiritually satisfying path.

Opportunities and Integration

Mindfulness and self-exploration can serve as gateways to spirituality in a secular world. This section delves into the practice of mindfulness and self-exploration and their potential benefits for reconnecting with one's spiritual self.

We discuss the importance of self-awareness and self-discovery as essential components of the spiritual journey. The guidance offers practical strategies for incorporating mindfulness and self-exploration into one's daily life to promote spiritual growth.

Human Connections and Empathy

In a secular world, fostering meaningful human connections and empathy can be a path to spirituality. This section explores the role of human relationships and empathy in spiritual fulfilment.

We discuss the challenges of cultivating empathy and authentic connections in a world focused on individualism. The guidance provides practical insights into building and nurturing relationships that support one's spiritual journey and promote a deeper sense of meaning and purpose.

Nurturing Spirituality in a Secular Context

In a secular world, individuals can create their own spiritual rituals and practices. This section delves into the importance of crafting personal rituals and practices that align with one's spiritual beliefs.

We discuss the significance of these rituals in providing a sense of structure and connection to one's spirituality. The guidance offers practical strategies for designing and incorporating personal rituals and practices into one's daily life.

Seeking Wisdom and Inspiration

Secularism does not exclude the search for wisdom and inspiration. This section explores the importance of seeking wisdom from various sources and finding inspiration in the world around us.

We discuss the challenges of navigating the information age and discerning valuable wisdom from noise. The guidance provides practical insights into seeking wisdom from diverse sources and finding inspiration in everyday experiences.

Embracing Spirituality in a Secular World

As we conclude this comprehensive guide on spirituality in a secular world, it's essential to recognize the transformative potential of embracing one's spirituality in a context that may not always encourage it. Spirituality is a deeply personal and meaningful journey, and it can coexist with secularism, even thrive within it.

The conclusion underscores the importance of making informed choices to nurture one's spirituality in a secular world. By incorporating the insights and strategies discussed in this guide, individuals can rediscover their sense of meaning and purpose, ultimately leading to a more spiritually connected, fulfilled, and balanced life.

Meditation and Ethical Living: Cultivating Virtue and Mindfulness

Meditation and ethical living are intimately connected, forming a foundation for a life of purpose, compassion, and mindfulness. This comprehensive guide explores the interplay between meditation and ethical principles, highlighting how meditation can support ethical living and vice versa. We delve into the core ethical principles and practical meditation techniques that promote virtue, compassion, and mindfulness in everyday life.

The Symbiotic Relationship Between Meditation and Ethics

The introduction sets the stage by highlighting the integral connection between meditation and ethical living. It emphasizes that ethical principles guide our actions, while meditation enhances our awareness and mindfulness, allowing us to live ethically and compassionately.

Core Ethical Principles

Ethical living is built upon core principles that guide our interactions and decisions. This section delves into these principles, including compassion, non-harming, honesty, and mindfulness.

We discuss the importance of these principles in shaping our ethical behaviours and promoting harmony in our relationships and the world. The guidance provides insights into how these principles serve as a moral compass for our lives.

Ethical Dilemmas and Decision-Making

Ethical dilemmas are a part of life, and how we navigate them speaks to our commitment to ethical living. This section explores the challenges of ethical decision-making and the role of mindfulness in resolving dilemmas.

We discuss real-life ethical challenges and the potential for confusion and inner conflict. The guidance offers practical strategies for using mindfulness and meditation to make ethical decisions that align with our values.

Loving-Kindness Meditation

Loving-kindness meditation, or Metta, is a powerful practice for cultivating compassion and promoting ethical living. This section delves into the practice of loving-kindness meditation and its potential to expand our capacity for love and kindness.

We discuss how this meditation can help us develop a sense of interconnectedness with all beings and foster a kind and compassionate heart. The guidance provides practical insights into incorporating loving-kindness meditation into your daily routine to support ethical living.

Mindfulness Meditation and Ethical Awareness

Mindfulness meditation plays a central role in ethical living by enhancing self-awareness and moral sensitivity. This section explores the practice of mindfulness meditation and its potential benefits for ethical awareness.

We discuss the role of mindfulness in recognizing and reframing unwholesome thoughts and behaviours. The guidance offers practical strategies for integrating mindfulness meditation into your daily life, fostering ethical living through conscious awareness.

Mindful Communication and Ethical Speech

Ethical speech is a fundamental aspect of ethical living. This section delves into the practice of mindful communication and its potential to enhance our ability to speak truthfully, kindly, and skilfully.

We discuss the challenges of practicing ethical speech in a world filled with distractions and impulsivity. The guidance provides practical insights into using mindfulness techniques to improve communication, ultimately promoting ethical living through conscious and compassionate speech.

Compassion in Action

Ethical living is not limited to meditation practice but extends to our actions in the world. This section explores the practical application of compassion in daily life.

We discuss how compassion can drive our actions, inspiring us to help others and contribute to a more ethical and harmonious world.

The guidance offers practical strategies for translating compassion into tangible acts of kindness and service.

Embracing Ethical Living Through Meditation

As we conclude this comprehensive guide on meditation and ethical living, it's essential to recognize the transformative potential of this symbiotic relationship. Meditation enhances our ethical awareness, and ethical living nurtures our meditation practice.

The conclusion underscores the importance of making informed choices to integrate meditation and ethical principles into our daily lives. By incorporating the insights and strategies discussed in this guide, individuals can cultivate a life of virtue, compassion, and mindfulness, ultimately leading to a more ethical, harmonious, and purposeful existence.

Finding Purpose and Meaning in a Fast-Paced Life: Navigating the Modern World with Clarity and Fulfilment

In today's fast-paced world, finding purpose and meaning is a universal pursuit. This comprehensive guide explores the complexities of living in a rapid and ever-changing society while seeking purpose and meaning. It offers insights and practical strategies for cultivating a deeper sense of purpose and meaning in daily life, even amidst the chaos and demands of the modern world.

The Pursuit of Purpose and Meaning in a Fast-Paced World

The introduction sets the stage by acknowledging the challenges of finding purpose and meaning in a world that often prioritizes speed and productivity. It emphasizes the importance of this pursuit for personal fulfilment and happiness.

The Modern Pace of Life

Modern life is characterized by its rapid pace, with constant demands on our time and attention. This section delves into the challenges of living in a fast-paced world and how this pace can affect our well-being and sense of purpose.

We discuss the impact of constant busyness, stress, and information overload on our ability to find purpose and meaning. The guidance provides insights into recognizing and addressing the negative effects of the modern pace of life.

The Search for Meaning in a Materialistic World

The modern world often emphasizes materialism and external achievements as markers of success. This section explores how this focus on material gains can impact our pursuit of meaning and purpose.

We discuss the challenges of navigating a value system that prioritizes wealth and status. The guidance offers practical strategies for reevaluating one's values and identifying sources of meaning beyond material success.

Self-Exploration and Self-Discovery

Self-exploration and self-discovery are essential for finding one's purpose and meaning in life. This section delves into the importance of understanding oneself and one's inner values.

We discuss the role of introspection and self-awareness in uncovering one's passions and strengths. The guidance provides practical insights into how to engage in self-exploration to align one's life with a deeper sense of purpose and meaning.

Living with Intention and Mindfulness

Living with intention and mindfulness can transform the way we engage with the world and find purpose. This section explores the practice of living mindfully and with a clear sense of purpose.

We discuss how intentionality and mindfulness can enhance our daily experiences and decision-making. The guidance offers practical strategies for incorporating mindfulness and intention into one's life to foster a greater sense of meaning and purpose.

Finding Purpose in Work and Career

For many, work is a significant aspect of life where purpose and meaning can be discovered. This section delves into the pursuit of meaningful and purposeful work.

We discuss the challenges of finding a fulfilling career in a fast-paced and competitive job market. The guidance provides practical insights into aligning one's career with one's values and passions, thereby discovering purpose and meaning in work.

Nurturing Relationships and Connection

Meaningful relationships and connection with others are vital for finding purpose in life. This section explores how nurturing relationships can contribute to a more meaningful existence.

We discuss the challenges of maintaining authentic connections in a world of digital communication and busyness. The guidance offers practical strategies for building and nurturing meaningful relationships that foster a deeper sense of purpose and meaning.

Embracing Purpose and Meaning in a Fast-Paced Life

As we conclude this comprehensive guide on finding purpose and meaning in a fast-paced life, it's essential to recognize the transformative potential of this pursuit. Even in a world that values speed and productivity, finding purpose and meaning is a fundamental and deeply human endeavour.

The conclusion underscores the importance of making informed choices to cultivate a life of purpose and meaning amidst the chaos and demands of the modern world. By incorporating the insights and strategies discussed in this guide, individuals can navigate the fast-paced life with clarity and fulfilment, ultimately leading to a more purposeful, meaningful, and balanced existence.

Your Journey Forward: Embracing Meditation for Modern Life

In the fast-paced and often overwhelming landscape of modern life, embracing meditation is a powerful choice, a journey toward a more balanced, centered, and harmonious existence. This guide explores the profound benefits of integrating meditation into your contemporary lifestyle, providing you with the tools to navigate the digital age with greater ease, reduce stress and anxiety, and discover inner peace and well-being. Your journey forward into the world of meditation for modern life begins with a series of fundamental steps.

Navigating the Modern Age

The introduction to your journey acknowledges the challenges and opportunities of living in the modern age. It recognizes the fast-paced, information-saturated, and digitally connected world that often contributes to stress, anxiety, and burnout. It highlights meditation as a powerful antidote, inviting you to embark on a transformative path of self-discovery and well-being.

Understanding the Essence of Meditation

Meditation is not a mystical or esoteric practice; it's a simple and profound technique that anyone can embrace. This section delves into the essence of meditation, explaining its core principles and demystifying any preconceived notions.

We discuss the importance of stillness, breath, and mindfulness in meditation. The guidance offers practical insights into grasping the essence of meditation as a tool for navigating modern life.

Creating Your Meditation Space

A dedicated meditation space is essential for your practice. This section explores the art of creating your meditation sanctuary, a place that promotes focus and tranquillity.

We discuss the challenges of finding space in a busy world and the potential benefits of a personal meditation space. The guidance provides practical strategies for establishing your meditation environment, no matter how small or modest.

Mindfulness Meditation: Staying Present in a Fast-Paced World

Mindfulness meditation is a fundamental technique for navigating the digital age. This section delves into the practice of mindfulness meditation and its potential to keep you present in a world filled with distractions.

We discuss the challenges of staying mindful in a fast-paced world and the benefits of mindfulness for reducing stress and anxiety. The guidance provides practical insights into incorporating mindfulness into your daily routine.

Breathing Techniques: Calming the Anxious Mind

Breathing techniques are powerful tools for managing stress and anxiety. This section explores the practice of various breathing techniques and their potential to calm the anxious mind.

We discuss the challenges of anxiety and its physical manifestations and the benefits of using breath as a calming anchor. The guidance provides practical strategies for integrating breathing techniques into your life for greater calm and resilience.

Digital Detox Meditation: Reclaiming Your Time and Attention

In a digital world, digital detox meditation is a valuable practice. This section delves into the technique of digital detox meditation and its potential to help you regain control over your time and attention.

We discuss the challenges of screen addiction and information overload and the benefits of disconnecting to reconnect with yourself. The guidance offers practical insights into using digital detox meditation to reclaim your life from the demands of the digital age.

Finding Time for Meditation in a Busy Schedule

In a busy schedule, finding time for meditation can be challenging but essential. This section explores the strategies for carving out space in your day for meditation.

We discuss the challenges of a packed routine and the potential benefits of making meditation a priority. The guidance provides practical strategies for creating small pockets of time for meditation, no matter how hectic your schedule.

Your Journey Forward

The conclusion to your journey forward in embracing meditation for modern life is a call to action. It underscores the transformative potential of meditation in reducing stress, anxiety, and burnout while fostering inner peace and well-being.

The conclusion emphasizes the importance of your commitment to this journey and encourages you to take the practical steps outlined in this guide. By incorporating the insights and techniques discussed, you can navigate the digital age with greater ease, reduce stress and anxiety, and embark on a path of self-discovery and well-being, ultimately leading to a more balanced, centered, and harmonious existence.

Navigating the Modern Maze - A Path to Wholeness and Wellness

In the hustle and bustle of modern life, the quest for well-being, balance, and peace often feels like an elusive dream. The digital age has ushered in unprecedented convenience and connectivity, yet it has also brought with it a unique set of challenges, including stress, anxiety, and burnout. This book, "Meditation for Modern Life: Overcoming Stress, Anxiety, and Burnout in the Digital Age," has been a journey through the intricacies of the modern maze, a path to wholeness and wellness in a world that sometimes seems designed to fragment our attention and shatter our inner peace.

As we conclude this exploration, let us take a moment to reflect on the core themes that have unfolded within these pages, and the transformative potential that meditation offers for those navigating the complexities of the digital age.

Reconnecting with the Self: The Essence of Meditation

Meditation, at its core, is a practice of reconnecting with the self. In the digital age, where external distractions and virtual interactions often dominate our lives, the need for this reconnection is greater than ever. Throughout this book, we have delved into the essence of meditation as a powerful tool for grounding oneself in the present moment. We've explored techniques such as mindfulness, deep breathing, and body scans, all of which serve as anchors in the fast-paced, ever-changing world.

The act of meditation is a simple yet profound return to the self. It is an acknowledgment of our inherent humanity and the recognition that amidst the digital noise, we possess an inner sanctuary of stillness and wisdom. By practicing meditation, we can nurture this sanctuary, fortify our resilience, and remain centered in the face of life's challenges.

The Digital Age Dilemma: Causes and Impact

In the initial chapters, we investigated the Digital Age Dilemma, uncovering the root causes of stress, anxiety, and burnout in the modern world. The relentless pace of life, the constant barrage of information, and the addictive allure of digital devices have all contributed to a state of perpetual distraction. These external forces exert a powerful influence on our well-being and threaten to undermine our sense of self.

By recognizing the unique challenges of the digital age, we can take a significant step toward reclaiming control over our lives. We've explored the impact of the digital age on our physical and mental health, underscoring the importance of safeguarding our well-being in this rapidly evolving landscape.

The Mind-Body Connection: How Stress Affects Your Health

The link between stress and health has been a recurring theme in our journey. Stress is not merely an emotional or mental burden; it has tangible, physiological effects on our bodies. Chronic stress can lead to a range of health issues, from heart problems to compromised immune function. Our exploration of the mind-body connection serves as a reminder of the imperative to manage stress and anxiety effectively.

By adopting meditation as a daily practice, we provide our bodies and minds with a valuable tool for mitigating the impact of stress. Meditation is not a means of escaping life's challenges but a way of fortifying ourselves to face them with resilience and equanimity. In doing so, we bridge the gap between the mind and body, cultivating a state of holistic well-being.

Recognizing the Signs of Stress, Anxiety, and Burnout

Throughout this book, we have offered insights into the signs and symptoms of stress, anxiety, and burnout. By recognizing these red flags in our lives, we can intervene early and take steps to regain balance and vitality. Understanding the unique ways that stress and anxiety manifest in the digital age equips us with the knowledge needed to address these challenges effectively.

In the chapters that delved into recognizing the signs of stress, we provided practical advice and self-assessment tools. This knowledge is instrumental in making informed decisions about our well-being and taking action to prevent burnout.

The Science of Meditation

The science of meditation has illuminated the transformative potential of this ancient practice. We have explored the extensive research into the physiological and psychological benefits of meditation. Scientific studies have revealed how meditation can positively impact our brains, reduce stress, improve mental clarity, and enhance emotional well-being.

Understanding the science behind meditation reinforces its legitimacy as a powerful tool for navigating the digital age. It offers a rationale for those who may be sceptical or hesitant to embrace meditation as a daily practice. By integrating scientific insights into our understanding of meditation, we align our efforts with the knowledge that has emerged from the rigorous scrutiny of the scientific community.

A Brief History and Overview

A brief history of meditation served as a foundational element in our journey. We traced the origins of meditation practices from ancient traditions, highlighting their enduring relevance in the modern age. Meditation is not a passing fad; it is a timeless practice that has adapted to the changing needs of humanity.

Our overview of meditation styles provided readers with a broad spectrum of options for exploring this practice. From mindfulness and loving-kindness meditation to body scan and walking meditation, we discovered an array of techniques that can be tailored to individual preferences and needs.

The Science Behind Meditation

Delving deeper into the science of meditation, we examined the physiological and psychological processes that occur during meditation. We explored how meditation affects the brain and body, leading to enhanced focus, reduced stress, and increased emotional resilience. This understanding reinforced the importance of making meditation a consistent part of our daily lives.

By unveiling the intricate ways in which meditation exerts its influence, we gained a deeper appreciation for the subtle yet profound changes that occur within us as we meditate. The interplay between the mind and body offers a fascinating lens through which to view the practice of meditation.

Tailored Meditation Techniques for Modern Life

In the heart of our journey, we explored tailored meditation techniques designed specifically for the challenges of modern life.

From digital detox meditation to finding time for meditation in a busy schedule, we offered practical strategies for integrating meditation into our daily routines. These techniques recognize the unique demands of the digital age and empower individuals to reclaim their time and attention.

The wide range of meditation practices cater to diverse needs and preferences, ensuring that there is a meditation style suitable for everyone. By tailoring our meditation approach to our individual circumstances, we create a path to wholeness that is both accessible and adaptable.

Beyond Meditation: Holistic Wellness

Beyond the practice of meditation, we considered the holistic aspects of wellness. We explored the role of nutrition, exercise, sleep, and social and emotional well-being in stress management. This holistic perspective recognizes that well-being is a multifaceted endeavour, and meditation is one piece of the puzzle.

Our exploration of these interconnected components of wellness underscored the importance of balancing physical health, emotional harmony, and social connections with meditation. By embracing a holistic approach, we empower ourselves to lead lives that are not just stress-free but also full of vitality and purpose.

Meditation and Ethical Living

In the concluding chapters, we delved into the profound connection between meditation and ethical living. We examined core ethical principles, ethical decision-making, and the practical application of meditation in nurturing compassion, kindness, and ethical awareness.

This exploration highlighted that meditation is not solely a means of personal well-being but a path to living ethically and contributing positively to the world. The interconnectedness between meditation and ethical living amplifies the transformative potential of the practice.

Finding Purpose and Meaning in a Fast-Paced Life

Our journey concluded with an exploration of finding purpose and meaning in a fast-paced life. We acknowledged the challenges of modernity and the influence of a materialistic world. Through self-exploration, mindfulness, and intentionality, we uncovered strategies for discovering a deeper sense of purpose and meaning in daily life.

This section reinforced that meditation is not a passive practice; it is a dynamic means of fostering personal growth, self-awareness, and purposeful living. By embracing meditation, individuals can navigate the modern age with clarity and fulfilment.

Your Journey Forward: Embracing Meditation for Modern Life

As we reflect on this journey through the pages of "Meditation for Modern Life," it is clear that meditation is not a destination but a journey forward. This journey is one of self-discovery, well-being, and mindful living. It is a path that acknowledges the challenges of the digital age and equips us with the tools to overcome them.

In your journey forward, I encourage you to embrace meditation as a daily practice. Find the meditation techniques that resonate with you and integrate them into your life. Recognize that the essence of meditation lies in its simplicity. It is an act of self-care and self-discovery that can be woven into the fabric of your day.

By dedicating time to meditation, you are investing in your well-being, resilience, and inner peace. You are aligning yourself with the enduring wisdom of ancient traditions while adapting to the demands of the modern world. You are, in essence, forging a path to wholeness and wellness in the digital age.

I thank you for accompanying me on this journey, and I encourage you to continue forward with the knowledge and practices you've acquired. May your path be one of ever-deepening mindfulness and fulfillment, not just for yourself but for the world you touch with your presence.

The digital age may bring challenges, but it also brings opportunities for profound personal transformation. In a world that often feels fragmented and fast-paced, meditation serves as a bridge to inner wholeness and wellness. It is a timeless practice that can guide us forward into the future with clarity and fulfilment.

About the Author

Aria Blake is a renowned wellness advocate, meditation instructor, and mindfulness expert whose journey has been marked by a deep commitment to helping individuals navigate the challenges of modern life. With a background in psychology and extensive training in meditation practices, Aria has dedicated her life to promoting well-being and balance in an increasingly fast-paced and digital world.

Aria's path to becoming an authority in the field of mindfulness and meditation was not just a professional choice but a deeply personal one. Her own encounters with stress, anxiety, and burnout in the digital age served as a catalyst for her exploration of meditation as a transformative tool. Aria's journey took her through diverse meditation traditions and techniques, each contributing to her rich understanding of the subject.

Having personally experienced the profound benefits of meditation, Aria felt a calling to share these insights with others. Her unique blend of modern insight and traditional wisdom has made her a sought-after speaker, meditation guide, and author. Aria is known for her ability to make meditation accessible and practical for individuals from all walks of life.

Through her books, talks, and workshops, Aria empowers people to embrace a daily meditation practice, offering them the tools they need to overcome stress, anxiety, and burnout. Her approach focuses on the integration of mindfulness into the fabric of daily life, equipping individuals to find inner peace and purpose amidst the challenges of the digital age.

Aria Blake's work is not just a reflection of her expertise but a testament to her passion for helping others lead healthier, more balanced lives. Her writings and teachings are marked by their authenticity, clarity, and the enduring belief that well-being is within everyone's reach. Aria is a guiding light in the modern wellness landscape, a voice of reason in a world that often seems chaotic, and a beacon of hope for those in search of serenity and fulfilment.